The Travel Agency Personnel Manual

by
Laurence Stevens

Volume 2

Merton House Publishing Company
Wheaton, Illinois

ISBN: 0-916032-04-3
Library of Congress Catalog Card Number: 78-60277

Copyright © 1979 by Merton House Publishing Company

All rights reserved. No part of this publication may be reproduced, stored in a retrieval system, or transmitted in any way or by any means, electrical, mechanical, photocopying, recording or otherwise, without written permission of the publisher, except for quotations made for the purposes of a review. All inquiries should be addressed to the publisher.

Merton House Publishing Company
937 West Liberty Drive
Wheaton, Illinois 60187
Manufactured in the United States of America

CONTENTS

Foreword v
Preface vii

Part 1 Recruiting Your Staff

1. Know What You are Searching for 1
2. Conducting a Job Interview 3
3. Good Traits and Danger Signals 9
4. How to Check References 11
5. The Final Evaluation 17
6. Hiring Travel School Graduates 19
7. Hiring the Agency Manager 22

Part 2 Managing Your Staff

8. How to Train Your Staff 25
9. How to Compensate Your Staff 33
10. Incentive and Profit-Sharing Programs 37
11. Wage and Hour Laws. Discrimination 40
12. How to Build and Maintain Morale 43
13. Evaluating Employee Performance 46
14. How to Give an Order 50
15. How to Take Disciplinary Action 53
16. How to Handle Employee Complaints 57
17. Dealing With the Problem Employee 59

Part 3 Managing Yourself

18. What Makes a Good Supervisor 63
19. The Manager's Responsibilities 66
20. Management Performance Self-Evaluation 69
    Appendix—A Travel Agency Policy Manual 75
    Index 80

FOREWORD

There has been, for a long time, a need for a systematic approach to the personnel needs of the travel industry. But, it is only during the past few years that the concepts of management theory and personnel administration have been formalized and applied to the business of the travel agent. While the travel industry is repeatedly acknowledged as being one of the most complex and changing businesses one can enter, until recently, it has been a disconnected chain of small, independent business locations, from an organizational and management point of view.

This manual is the first successful effort to establish for travel agency owners and managers the principles and practices by which to select, hire, supervise, and motivate their staff. While matters of personnel selection and administration have always been of importance to those heading business organizations, this has, until now, been treated in a cavalier fashion by most travel agencies. These processes have existed without direction and orientation and frequently been counter-productive to the hiring agency. The rapid growth of the travel services, combined with the increasing public demand for professional travel counseling, has resulted in a great increase in the number of jobs created. This expanding number of people being placed in travel sales positions requires a more orderly and methodical approach to the subject.

Several areas of concern need to be addressed by those individuals in positions which affect the destiny of their travel business and the course of other people's lives.

First, it is not what you can do yourself, but what you can get accomplished through the efforts of others that counts. Most supervisors and managers have "come up through the ranks." They have previously been the line workers who have been recognized for their efforts and are given the responsibility and authority for hiring others. It frequently takes a long time for such a doer to become a delegator.

The newcomer to the area of these responsibilities must remember that he or she must be free to accomplish the managerial and administrative duties which maintain and perpetuate the travel agency—not be performing the daily activities for which someone else is being hired.

Second, there is need for a competency based model for the selection of staff for a particular travel agency and job. To the person on the street, the term travel agent means only one thing: The person who plans trips. But, to those in the industry, the title has numerous meanings. One travel operation is not necessarily similar to another and the requirements of each may differ considerably. It is frequently easy to select a job applicant based on gut feelings. This, unfortunately, is what is frequently done in the small business where the management is unprepared or untrained for the selection process. Here the perception that the applicant will fit in and is capable overrides the need for a formalized approach to hiring. The standards and criteria for employee selection of travel counselors for specific operations need to be more than vague, personal perceptions. There needs to be recognition and documentation of the requirements for the positions for which interviews are being conducted. A counter sales person requires different personality traits and background than an employee scheduling tours or filing literature. And these differ considerably from someone wishing to be an outside sales representative. But all may be called "travel agent" by various companies. This text offers an organized approach to these areas.

Then, there is motivation: the key to employee satisfaction and productivity. The tenets of considerable research and application are suggested here. For, once having hired an employee to do the work, owners and managers must realize that it is their actions which affect the attitude and motivation of those who have been hired. If an employee goes home after work and kicks the cat, it is most likely due to the frustration and anxiety produced in some way on the job. After all, employee production, based upon a positive attitude toward the business, co-workers, and the products and services being sold, is the key to both customer and management satisfaction.

While most people reading this book may be, at least in part, familiar with the concepts set forth, some parts and their application to the travel agency will be new. By following the principles and procedures stated here, the transition to a recognized supervisor of travel people will be made easy. Your personal abilities in the areas of personnel selection and administration will be translated into success for your business. This, in turn, will attract more capable and qualified applicants who want to be part of such an acknowledged team of professionals.

Scott Feinerman
Professor of Tourism and Travel
Los Angeles Airport College Center

PREFACE

If you manage or own a travel agency, your personal success as well as the growth, efficiency, and ultimately, the profitability of the agency are determined not only by your own skills and leadership qualities, but also by the caliber of the employees you supervise. The most important person in any travel agency is the manager. The next most important asset is a well-trained and a highly motivated staff. An agency can be well financed, own expensive furniture and fixtures, have professionally decorated premises and occupy prestigious office space, but if the manager is mediocre and the staff incompetent and badly trained, you can be certain that at best such an agency will barely break even and at worst will soon go out of business.

The secret to success in the highly competitive retail travel agency business is a well-trained, aggressive and knowledgeable manager, and a well-trained and highly motivated staff, all of whom operate at a high level of performance with high morale. I have seen all too many agencies fail—not because of finances, but simply because management and staff were incompetent. Experience does not necessarily guarantee competence, nor does it guarantee that a person possesses management capabilities. Too many agency owners tend to hire the cheapest manager they can find, and pay their employees as little as possible. It's little wonder that these agencies experience high turnover of staff and soon go out of business.

As it is people, and not money, that eventually brings about growth and, therefore, profits, it is wise to invest heavily in those who are responsible for operating the agency. "Invest" in this instance does not mean a cash outlay, (although it generally follows that the more you are prepared to pay in terms of salaries and benefits, the higher quality of employees you attract), but relates to how well the staff is trained, supervised, and above all, how they are motivated. My philosophy of life is that if I have to spend anything from eight to twelve hours a day earning my bread then I am going to *like* what I'm doing. People should *enjoy* their jobs to the point that what they do is not "work" but is creative, enjoyable and personally fulfilling.

Apart from hiring only top-notch people in the first place, it is absolutely *essential* to keep them happy once you have them. An agency with high morale is a happy, thriving place and a joy to be in. Such an agency isn't hard to spot: the employees are happy, content, well paid and they know their jobs. Work is fun. The clientele is steady and growing, and, because of the competency of the agency, new clients are continually being referred by satisfied clients.

This book, then, is for and about people in travel. More specifically, it was written for the retail travel agent. Much of the material is just plain, good old common sense, and perhaps you will be familiar with many of the topics covered. But some sections might be new to you. Take the time to read and study the book thoroughly, and then apply what you have learned to your own agency. There are no tricks to good supervision, but there *are* right and wrong ways of hiring, supervising and handling other people.

The Travel Agency Personnel Manual is in three distinct parts: The first section deals with recruiting your staff; the second section explains how to handle and supervise those under you, while the last segment covers what makes a good manager and how to be one. While each section covers a different aspect of management, each is indivisibly related to each of the others and as such cannot be separated.

Every effort has been made to condense the material as much as possible without losing the point of the subject matter. The writing is also primarily in the male gender. This is not because I'm a chauvanist (because I'm not), but because it is impossible to switch back and forth between "his" and "her" situations. I can assure you that there is no intent to discriminate. As everyone knows, or should know, women make up a larger percentage of travel agency employees than do men. Women have contributed enormously to the growth and success of the retail travel agency field, and I don't know where the industry would be without them. Quite frankly, I have found that, after running agencies of all sizes, women often do a much better job than men. Perhaps this is because women usually can relate better to all of the detail work than men. In any event, all situations described apply equally to a woman.

Let *The Travel Agency Personnel Manual* help you to become a better supervisor. Use it in your office. Refer to it next time you hire someone or have an employee-related problem in your office.

Laurence Stevens

PART 1
Recruiting Your Staff

1. KNOW WHAT YOU ARE SEARCHING FOR

If you supervise others, it is inevitable that sooner or later you will have a vacancy to fill in your office. A vacancy can occur in a number of different ways, but it is most likely that you will have to replace someone who left your employ or who was promoted to another position, or because the agency is expanding and you have to increase your staff. Should you hire the wrong person, it might take you some time to (a) first discover your mistake, and (b) muster up courage to fire him. Making a mistake in hiring a new employee means that you will have to start the hiring process all over again *after* you have expended valuable salary dollars. The smaller the agency, the fewer errors you can afford when it comes to hiring new employees. It is not always a simple matter to select the right person—especially if you interview only once or twice a year. Even the most seasoned of professional personnel recruiters makes his share of mistakes, as it is never possible to be absolutely certain about a new employee. It often happens that someone who (on the surface) appears to be a rational, industrious and well-adjusted individual, becomes a nightmare because of problems the interviewer was not aware of *and had not discovered prior to hiring.*

While it is essential to fill a current position with a qualified applicant, and thereby solve the immediate staffing problem, you must also take the future into consideration. When you do hire, it is necessary to choose someone whom you believe will respond to your training, leadership and guidance, but the candidate should also have the potential to be able to assume greater responsibilities in the months and years ahead. Try to project where your agency will be one or two years into the future, and judge where a new employee will fit in then.

When we talk about the selection of staff we mean just that—*choice*. If you have one applicant for your position you cannot select but only decide if he is capable of performing the job. Try to line up a minimum of three applicants for every job opening so you can make a true selection.

SKILLS INVENTORY CHECKLIST

Next time you interview or hire, run down this list and use it to check off the skills the applicant must have.

Skill or function   *Experience required*

Domestic ticketing
International ticketing
Groups/incentives/conventions
Cruise sales
Domestic sales
International sales
FIT planning
Auto rentals
Railroad bookings
Package tour sales
Fares and rate computations
Letter writing
Ticket reports
Accounting
Making sales calls
Answer general inquiries
Typing
Planning sales promotions
Other)
Other)
Other) Add other skills required
Other) for the specific job.
Other)
Other)

If you can only find one applicant with the qualifications you need, you will have to decide on whether to hire him or to risk losing him to a competitor while you look around for more candidates. If good travel staff are at a premium and are hard to come by in your area, you had better go ahead and hire your applicant, providing that (1) he has all of the skills required, (2) is likely to be compatible, and (3) the references check out to your satisfaction.

If you use one of the few employment agencies which specialize in travel staff, you will find that the applicant has already been carefully prescreened and selected by the agency to fit your particular job opening. It is usually unnecessary to interview more than one applicant, because the agency has already performed most of the important recruiting functions for you.

If you have not drawn up a job description you should take the time to you have a clear picture of all of the skills and qualifications required to perform the job. To put it another way: You must fit the applicant to the job you have to fill and not adjust the job to the applicant.

If you have not drawn up a job description, you should take the time to do so, as you will find it much easier to match up applicants if you have prepared guidelines. It is not necessary to write up a lengthy characterization of the specifications, and a few notes jotted on one side of the paper will generally be adequate. However, if you have the time to do so, do take a little more time and make a list consisting of the basic functions and responsibilities of the job so that you can check them off as you interview each applicant or review the application form. If you have a detailed job description, you can also use it as a measuring tool to supervise not only the job itself but the occupant who holds it.

List also the qualifications and skills the applicant must possess as a prerequisite for consideration for the job. For instance, do you want a younger person, or do you prefer someone with maturity? How much education and how many years of experience in travel? Does he meet the management experience requirements as defined by ATC and IATA? Do you want someone to fill an immediate opening, or must the applicant also have potential for promotion at a future date?

You can use the Skills Inventory Checklist to help you prepare a job description. While it includes many of the more essential skills, you should add others that are important to your own situation and the position you have to fill.

Remember:

DESPERATION HIRING = PERSPIRATION SUPERVISION

2. CONDUCTING A JOB INTERVIEW

The actual interview is the means by which the employer and the applicant meet to look over one another. Before you reach this point it is a good idea to try to study the employment application or résumé so you can determine those areas which require further investigation or clarification. Make notes to yourself so you can cover questionable areas during the interview.

By the time you reach the interview stage, you should have talked with applicants on the telephone, weeded out those who are obviously unqualified, and selected those who appear to have the experience and qualifications required to perform the job. Depending upon the job itself, the number of applicants, and the amount of time available before you must make a decision, you might want to hold two interviews with each qualified applicant.

The Preliminary Interview

The preliminary interview (should you conduct one) is really nothing more than an additional elimination process designed to reject those who are unqualified, and to select those who are to be considered as prime candidates. If you do conduct a preliminary interview, it should be kept as brief as possible, and fifteen or twenty minutes at the most is sufficient time to determine serious interest.

In the preliminary interview, all you need to do is review the duties of the job and what you expect from the person who holds it. Explain the company benefits and starting salary, and then try to discover if the applicant is capable of performing the job as you have described it. Perhaps he will not even be interested in the job when he finds out more about it, and the preliminary interview will help you to discover his attitude towards it.

It is important to reach a decision as to the status of the applicant so that you can tell him if he is to be considered for the job or not. Let him know that you will contact him again in a couple of days. If the applicant obviously is not what you want, then be frank and tell him so during this interview. It is unfair to let him think he is in the running for the job when he will not even be considered. Being honest with him will eliminate further contact and permit him to seek other opportunities for which he might be better qualified.

How to Conduct a Successful Job Interview

There is a right and a wrong way to conduct an interview, and since each method takes about the same length of time, it is a good idea to get into the habit of hiring your new employees the correct way.

The first golden rule of interviewing:

Never conduct an interview until you have studied the employment application or résumé in advance.

This will allow you the opportunity to make notes on questions you want to ask and will alert you to gaps in employment and other possible danger signals.

The Location. Establishing Rapport

Try to conduct job interviews in as private a location as you can, and avoid the interruptions of telephone calls and visitors. If privacy is a problem—as it is in most smaller travel agencies—then you might want to consider interviewing applicants outside of normal office hours or even informally away from the office premises, perhaps over a cup of coffee.

If the interview is to be successful, the applicant must feel comfortable, relaxed and uninhibited, so establish an easy relationship right from the start. You, as the interviewer and employer, must set the scene for a smooth two-way conversation where there is free-flowing discussion on both sides. Bear in mind that many people are naturally nervous when they go on a job interview, so try to compensate for this. If your applicant is tense and reticent, then the objectiveness of the job interview will be defeated, and you will have difficulty in performing a satisfactory evaluation.

Appearance of the Applicant. Tardiness

Generally speaking, the first impression we get of someone at the initial meeting tends to stay with us. Observe if the applicant is neatly dressed, shoes shined, suit pressed, etc. If a female, look at her grooming, neatness of hair, make-up applied properly and so on. How a person is groomed can be an important indicator to the interviewer. If there is a tendency towards sloppiness and untidyness in dress and appearance, this could perhaps indicate that these traits might possibly carry over into work habits.

Observe promptness. If the applicant was late in keeping the appointment with you, find out why. There could be any number of legitimate reasons, but if tardiness *is* a trait, you should know *before* you hire and not afterwards.

What Does the Applicant Want

This is the time for you to listen and discover as much as you can about why he wants or needs a job. You can accomplish this by encouraging him to talk to you about previous jobs, his experiences in travel, why he thinks he is qualified for your job and what he knows about the function of the job.

If you cannot get him to loosen up and talk freely, then you will have to embark upon a question and answer session to get the facts, though it is preferable to let him talk independently but with you guiding the conversation. If you are alert, and if you listen carefully to what he has to say, you should be able to get a good knowledge of the applicant and learn if he will fit your job opening.

Tell What You Have to Offer

Now it is your turn, and the best thing to do at this point is to cover the job in detail and explain the performance expected. Cover the starting salary range and when you would normally expect to review the salary. Outline any bonus or profit sharing plans you have, and go on to describe your health insurance benefits, your policy on allotment of IATA and ATC passes, familiarization trips—in fact everything an applicant needs to know about the job and your agency.

If there are any negative aspects of the position (and all jobs have them), be certain to mention them. But above all, be factual and realistic, because if you over-glamorize the job to a new or potential employee, he will tend to become unhappy when he finds out that the job and work conditions were not as represented to him during the interview. In the scramble to find qualified staff, an overly anxious manager can easily—perhaps unintentionally—use alluring tactics to land a desirable applicant. But once an employee thinks he has been "had" then he might start looking somewhere else, and then you will have to start the hiring process all over again after you have wasted time and all-too-valuable salary dollars.

Invite Questions

Employment is a two-way street. Management is seeking a loyal and efficient employee, and the applicant is looking for a good place to work, security, a fair salary with potential for increases, and of course all of the fringe benefits that go into working in the travel agency field. So invite questions from your job applicant, because you will learn a great deal about him by the type of questions he asks.

For example, are the majority of the questions about salary, vacation policy, passes, benefits, etc. (or what you can do for him)? Or does he probe into your agency and ask questions about the job, any sales quotas and performance expected? If he tends to confine his questioning to job benefits and compensation, then you *might* consider this to be a danger signal and use caution before you hire. But if his questions are balanced between what he can expect to receive in terms of compensation and benefits, against requirements of the job and what you expect of him, then he is considering and weighing the entire situation.

Ask Your Own Questions

As you listen and talk with your applicants make mental, or preferably written, notes on questions you want to ask. When you do ask questions, try to phrase them in such a manner that requires more than a yes or no answer. A specific question should enable you to obtain the information you need without delay.

Your questions would normally follow this pattern:

1. Questions raised from reading the employment application or résumé. Includes questions surrounding obvious gaps in employment, education, personal data, etc.
2. Questions that come to your attention as you listen to the applicant talk.

3. Questions about the applicant's professional knowledge, ability and previous experience.
4. Questions on the applicant's loyalty, goals and opinions.

The following checklist will be helpful to you as a nucleus of questions. There will be many others, and you will have to adjust your questioning to fit the job as well as the applicant.

Describe your present (or previous) responsibilities.
How do you spend an average day?
What did you enjoy most about your last job?
What did you dislike most about your last job?
Did you get along well with your supervisor?
Describe the supervisor's supervisory methods.
Did you get along well with your colleagues?
Do you usually get along with people?
What do you know about our company (agency)?
Why did you apply for our job?
Why, exactly, did you leave your previous job(s)?
Did you receive promotions and salary increases?
Do you know domestic airline ticketing?
Do you know international airline ticketing?
How long have you been able to write domestic/international tickets?
Which tariffs can you use?
Have you ever attended a tariff and ticketing seminar?
Can you complete the ticket report?
Have you ever been on board a cruise ship?
Which domestic resort areas have you visited?
Which foreign countries have you visited?
Have you ever been on a familiarization trip? Where?
With which areas are you familiar and which do you sell best?
Which tour operator do you favor for Europe, (Hawaii, S. America, etc.)?
Whom do you use for your FIT's?
Do you compose and write all your own letters?
Do you know your annual sales figure?
If you don't know the answer to a question, what do you do?
Would you sell a client a tour or package in which you did not believe?
What are your hobbies?
Do you mind working overtime?
Can you get to our office easily from where you live?

In school or college: Did you enter competitive sports, were you ever elected as a club officer or team leader?
Do you mind routine?
How do you react to criticism?
What are your long-term goals?
What type of position do you want to be in five years from now?
Describe some of the problems you solved in your last job.

For Managers

    Do you enjoy making decisions?
    Do you delegate, or prefer to handle everything yourself?
    Do you enjoy new challenges?
    Describe your method of getting the job done?
    What was the most innovative idea you created?
    How did you persuade the manager to accept the idea?

The manner in which your applicants answer questions such as these will reveal much. Look carefully for signs of dissatisfaction with previous jobs and with former supervisors. Too many complaints about previous or current jobs, or an abundance of petty gripes, might indicate a chronic complainer who could quite possibly create future problems for you.

Look for a positive attitude, ambition and drive, initiative, self-motivation, the desire to acquire new skills and to accept new responsibilities.

Concluding the Interview

By the time you conclude the interview, you should have a good idea of the applicant's personal background, education, hobbies, skills, and his actual on-the-job experience that would either qualify or disqualify him. If he is a serious candidate, then tell him so, and let him know when he can expect to hear from you. If you do not consider him to be among your list of active applicants, let him know at the conclusion of the interview. Tell him that you appreciate his time and interest but that you do have other applicants who have more experience than he does.

The good interviewer:

    Is objective.
    Knows in advance what questions he needs to ask.
    Listens well.
    Explains the job thoroughly.
    Confines the discussion to interviewing.
    Knows exactly what he wants.
    Informs the applicant where he stands.

The poor interviewer:

    Has only a vague idea of the applicant he seeks.
    Is subjective.
    Plays the interview "by ear."
    Is not clear about the job or its requirements.
    Has too much to say. (About himself and the company.)
    Cannot decide—always wants to see one more applicant.

3. GOOD TRAITS AND DANGER SIGNALS
SOME GOOD TRAITS TO LOOK FOR

Each of us is endowed with both good and bad traits in our personalities. Some we are born with (inherited), and others we pick up as we proceed through life (acquired). It goes without saying that when you hire staff, you would be wise to select only those who possess as many good traits as possible. But take note of the fact that the chances of locating a candidate with nothing *but* good qualities is next to impossible.

As you evaluate job applicants, satisfy yourself that those who are under serious consideration for the job have as many of the following characteristics as possible:

Friendliness

He gets along with his fellow workers, the clients and the suppliers with whom he does business on a day-to-day basis. In fact, he can get along with just about anyone, and he enjoys serving and helping people.

Positive Mental Attitude and Enthusiasm

These two characteristics generally go together. The better the outlook and attitude a person has, the better he will perform at his job. A person might have an abundance of skills and technical knowledge of travel, but if enthusiasm is absent, all you can expect is that he will just do the job and no more.

Self-Motivation

He should be capable of working without close supervision once he has learned the job and the responsibilities that go along with it. A self-motivated person will usually do more than is asked or expected, and when he runs out of work he will either ask for something to do or will take it upon himself to find tasks requiring attention and completion. He is always busy and enjoys keeping his nose to the grindstone.

Systematic

He is versatile and speaks and writes clearly so that he cannot possibly be misunderstood. He has developed his own system for getting the job done, and is interested in his employer, as well as the clients. He is sensitive to the needs of people, is able to keep his temper under control, is stable, and has creative ideas.

Ambitious

He is anxious to get ahead, and will eagerly accept any assignment he is given with a cheerful attitude. He wants promotion and progress, and will work hard to achieve his goals and ambitions.

Honesty and Reliability

He can be trusted in every way, and gains a reputation for doing what he says he is going to do. He is always on time for appointments, is at his desk early, and always seems to be around when you need him most. He will competently handle anything given to him, but will always go to his supervisor for advice and guidance if necessary. He can be trusted to handle cash, tickets and other valuables.

DANGER SIGNALS

The trained recruiter and personnel specialist refers to this as the "red flag" zone. If you interview only once or twice a year, or sporadically, it is easy to overlook certain characteristics in an applicant that would set off alarm bells in someone who interviews and recruits regularly.

Red flags can show up almost anywhere—in the employment application, during the interview, or when you start checking out the references. Whenever and wherever they appear, they must be treated seriously and thoroughly investigated. But remember that each of us is endowed with red flag characteristics, and when you come across them in an applicant, you will have to judge if they are ones with which you can live. Don't let one or two red flags deter you from hiring what might be an outstanding employee.

However, if there is a history of problems or red flags, then proceed with caution, because you are inviting possible problems later. If you run up five or more red flags in any one applicant, better look somewhere else, because no matter how badly you want to fill the opening, you cannot afford to do so with the wrong person—in fact it is better not to hire *anyone* than to hire a potential risk who might cause you endless trouble.

To help you to pinpoint danger areas, a list of some of the more important red flags follow. However, not every one should be considered a danger signal in every applicant. For example, a heavy foreign accent that would perhaps be a liability to a commercial desk would probably be a decided asset for a foreign or international counselor position. (An accent adds credibility to the discussion of foreign destinations.) Weigh each factor carefully and *individually,* then apply them in the context of each applicant to see if they will seriously hinder an applicant's job performance or result in you having to spend too much valuable time in supervision.

Possible Red Flags

    Too many jobs
    Unable (or refusal) to account for all time since leaving school or college
    Minimum education for the job
    Insufficient knowledge and/or skills for the job
    Most recent earnings are higher than you can offer
    Has been unemployed for a long period of time
    Has ever been fired from a job. (In all fairness to the applicant, you owe it to both him and yourself to find out exactly why he was terminated.)

Did not finish high school
Dropped out of college
Frequent change of residence
Physical disabilities. (Only consider these if they will interfere with job performance.)
A history of frequent illness
Too many dependents for the salary you offer
Too many debts
Did not like his previous manager or supervisor
If a female applicant, small children which might require her to be absent if children become ill. (Note carefully that this is not a valid reason to refuse employment but is mentioned merely as an example to alert you to possible problems.)
Dissatisfied with advancement or salary increases
Illogical reason(s) for leaving previous job(s)
Unwilling to travel. (If the applicant is married and the job requires travel, better satisfy yourself that there are no objections to traveling.)
A recent divorce or separation
Dishonorable discharge from the service
A prison record
Has a record of financial, gambling or drinking problems

These are just a few of red flags to look for and are only a representation of hundreds of problem areas of which to beware.

ONE OR TWO RED FLAGS: OK—we all have some
THREE OR FOUR RED FLAGS: Proceed with caution
FIVE OR MORE RED FLAGS: Don't hire—you're asking for trouble

4. HOW TO CHECK REFERENCES

Checking out the references of the candidate in whom you are seriously interested is probably the most important single step in the entire hiring process. When you check references, you are verifying the truthfulness of the information and data provided by the applicant in his application. You will also get (hopefully) an objective opinion as to the ability, worth and honesty of your applicant from those for whom he worked previously.

All too often, small employers—including many travel agents—fail to take the time to perform even the most cursory of reference checks, and so expose themselves to a variety of hazards and possible financial losses which could easily be avoided with a couple of telephone calls.

Never hire anyone until you have personally checked all references.

Engrave these words on your mind and never forget them. It will cost you a few minutes of your time to discover any existing problems, and if you do it before you hire someone, you might save yourself a considerable amount of money in terms of payroll expense.

TELEPHONE REFERENCE CHECK

Name of applicant _____ date _____

Name of employer _____

Name of supervisor _____ tel. no. _____

1. When did he work for you? From _____ to _____
2. What were his final earnings? ($_____ per_____)
3. Why did he leave your employ?
4. Would you rehire?
5. Was his attendance good?
6. Was he punctual?
7. Did he produce for you?
8. Were his sales average, above average, or below average?
9. Did he get along well with others in the office?
10. Did he get along well with you?
11. Did he have any drinking, dope or gambling problems?
12. Are his morals good?
13. Did he have any financial problems?
14. Did he have any marital or emotional problems?
15. Can he work without supervision?
16. Is he self motivated?
17. Is he honest?
18. Is he accurate?

Reference checking will protect you in several other ways. For example, if you need an international consultant, you must satisfy yourself that the applicant has the capabilities of performing the duties and responsibilities required for this position. While an applicant might *say* he can do the job, there should be a great deal of doubt if all he has ever done is book domestic packages with perhaps a sprinkling of foreign bookings thrown in.

Each one of us is anxious to upgrade ourselves in status and earnings, but a vacancy must be filled on actual *abilities* and *experience,* not on *desires* and *goals.*

When you check references is also important—timing is vital. For example, it is too late to start checking references *after* an applicant is on the payroll and handling tickets, clients and reservations. The job of checking references is part of, and has a specific place in, the total hiring process. You might even want to get much of the spade work out of the way before you interview, so you can be one jump ahead of the applicant and thus ask him to clarify those points which require an explanation or clarification.

If you do your checking after the interview, you will have formed a personal opinion of the applicant and will also be able to probe into questions occurring during the interview.

There are pros and cons to each method, but however you prefer to handle it, just be sure to get an objective report from previous employers, so that you can put everything together and arrive at an overall judgment.

TYPES OF REFERENCE CHECKS

There are two types of reference checks: Oral (telephone) and written (letter). The telephone inquiry is generally the most satisfactory of the two, because if there *are* any problems in an applicant's background, the probability of discovering them through a letter are unlikely. Most employers don't mind providing oral references over the telephone, but many balk at divulging anything more than basic information in a written communication—especially if they are prone to giving a poor reference.

Now this does not mean that you should never use a letter; there are times you will have to do so. For example, if an applicant's previous employment was several years ago, and perhaps a couple of thousand miles away, then you could get away with sending the employer a letter requesting specific information. But be prepared to follow up with a phone call, should the reply indicate that there were problem areas.

The Telephone Reference Check

The Telephone Reference Check format can be used when you make this check. Most of the essential questions are included, but you should add others as they relate to the applicant and the job. Have all questions in front of you before you make the call. If you follow this format, and then include your own questions, you should have no difficulty in acquiring a great deal of information with minimum effort.

When you make the call, identify yourself immediately, and say that you wish to verify employment information given to you by your applicant. It is best to go directly to the applicant's immediate superior, because the response you would normally receive from the personnel department will be stock answers and will not usually include the more specific and detailed information you need about performance and habits. While you will want to verify the truthfulness of the data in the employment application, it is essential to also obtain the views and evaluations from someone who actually knew and supervised your applicant.

Assure the employer that any information given to you will remain strictly confidential (and make certain it does). Should you have to turn down your applicant, based on information given to you in confidence by a previous employer, never let the applicant know it. To do so could cause a problem for someone who was gracious and considerate enough to reveal facts essential to an evaluation.

Once in a while you will come up against an employer who is unwilling to reveal any information other than that your applicant was in his employ. Often the reason for such reticence is that the employer is unsure of exactly who is calling. If he has any doubts, you can suggest that he take your number and call *you*—this should convince him about the legitimacy of the call.

Some employers—especially the larger companies—have a policy of refusing to give out *any* information. If you run into such a situation, you will have to go up the ladder to perhaps more than one manager or supervisor until you find one who is willing to give you the information you need, or at the very least confirm employment dates, salary and the reason for leaving the company.

If the employer refuses to give you *any* information, you can remind him that if he were doing the hiring, he would refuse to employ a key person unless he were able to obtain several satisfactory references, and that all you are doing is asking for the same courtesy and consideration he would expect. If you are polite, but persistent, you should be able to obtain most of the information you need to make an assessment and evaluation, and arrive at a decision as to whether to hire or not.

Hidden Meanings

As you proceed down your checklist, listen carefully to the tone and inflection of the voice of the speaker. The manner in which your questions are answered will often convey far greater meaning than a direct response.

Probably the most meaningful question you can ever ask an employer is, "Would you rehire?" It is a leading question and one which will, when answered, give you a good insight into the relationship between the employer and your applicant. A quick and decisive, "Yes, I would," will usually indicate that the applicant is in good standing with his previous employer. However, if you receive a hesitant or an evasive answer, you will have to pursue the point until you are able to get a more definitive response.

An employer will often try to evade a direct answer because while he does not want to rehire the applicant, neither does he want to impair an opportunity or injure the career of someone who once worked for him. He gets around the question by saying something like, "It's not our policy to rehire former staff." You then must discover that if it *were* their policy, would they then rehire.

Objectivity

When an employer gives a reference on a former employee, it should be objective and based upon the professional ability and competence of the individual at performing his job. Unfortunately, some employers tend to base their appraisal on a personal like or dislike of the person.

If the references you get are negative, or indicate problems, you must be certain that the employer is being objective. An employer might, for example, be resentful about someone who left his employ and perhaps caused him inconvenience. Perhaps there was a personality conflict, but if you think the employer is unfair in his reference take another look at the application as a guideline. If the applicant was employed for any length of time and has a history of salary increases and perhaps increased responsibility, the chances are that he did a pretty good job.

If there is more than one employer, make a point of contacting each of them, because while you might get a marginal reference from one, you might get an entirely different evaluation—good or bad—from another.

Discrepancies

If there are differences between the information the applicant has put on his application and that furnished by the employer, consider this to be a danger area, and start probing deeper. It could quite easily be an honest mistake, as your applicant might have had a lapse of memory when it came to exact employment dates—especially if the employment was several years previously. But it could also be a deliberate attempt to mislead you and done in the hope that you would not check too closely. You will then have to determine if it was an honest error or a genuine deception tactic. If you do come across variances, by all means confront your applicant with them, but reserve judgment until you have all of the facts.

Accounting for All Time

Have your applicant give you employment dates which include the *month* as well as the year of employment commencement or termination. All time should be accounted for since leaving school or college. Do not settle for an evasive "Oh, I just cannot remember" answer, but insist that he take the time and effort to remember. If he cannot do so during the interview, ask him to call you the next day. You should then verify all dates with previous employers, and if *they* cannot remember, request them to check their records.

SUGGESTED REFERENCE LETTER TO BE SENT TO PREVIOUS EMPLOYERS
(use your letterhead with reply paid envelope)

_____ has applied for a position with us, and in order to reach a decision, we would be most appreciative if you would furnish us with the information requested below and return it in the enclosed envelope at your earliest convenience. We assure you that all information will be treated in a strictly private and confidential manner, and will not be divulged to anyone.

Date employed: _____ Date of termination: _____

Position: _____ Salary at termination: _____

Reason for termination: _____

_____

Would you re-hire? _____ if not, why? _____

_____

Did he perform the job: Well? _____ Fair? _____ Poorly _____

Was he accurate in his work? _____ Did he produce well? _____

How was his attendance? _____ Was he usually prompt? _____

Did he get along well with you? _____ With his colleagues? _____

What are his strong points? _____

_____

What are his weak points? _____

_____

Are you aware of any financial, marital or emotional problems? _____ If so please describe _____

Is he honest? _____ Please furnish below other comments and opinions that will help us in our evaluation:

_____

_____

Date _____ Signed _____

Position _____

Written References

The amount and quality of information you can obtain in a written reference is negligible compared to that you can get from a telephone conversation. In fact, many employers will not commit themselves in a written reference but will do so on the telephone. If you just sit down and write a letter to an employer and request a written evaluation, chances are you will never hear from him. Make your request in a manner to which the recipient will find easy to reply—so simple, in fact, that he could hardly avoid not responding. Use your letterhead and type up a list of questions to which you want answers, but be sure to leave plenty of space for additional comments. Enclose a postage-paid return envelope and use the suggested sample letter.

Personal References

Most employment applications have space for an applicant to include names and addresses of people who know him at the personal level—outside of his work and profession. While most employers do check them out, you might want to bear in mind that an applicant is not about to give you the names of people who might give him a poor reference. There are pros and cons to using these references, but if you have a marginal applicant, it is still a good idea to contact one or two of the references on the list. The chances of obtaining an *objective* reference from someone who is probably a personal friend is pretty remote.

5. THE FINAL EVALUATION

The final step in the hiring process is the evaluation of each candidate and the selection of one of them. Based upon the knowledge you have gained through interviews and reference checking, there are several final factors you must consider before making the all-important final decision.

Does He Have the Knowledge

No matter what the job is, the person you hire must possess the necessary knowledge and experience required to perform it well. If the applicant is marginal in knowledge for the position but has good potential, then you will have to decide if you are willing to accept potential or hold out for more experience, and whether the applicant *must* have this experience as a prerequisite to hiring. If you know exactly what you want in skills, you can assure yourself that the applicants do have the necessary credentials in order to be seriously considered for the job.

Will He be Happy in the Job

You must be careful not to oversell the job during the interview. Unless the employee enjoys his work, he will lean towards dissatisfaction, and will perhaps perform below his capacity. Will the salary you offer be adequate, or will he soon be asking for an increase? (Look at his previous earnings record.) Is your office easy to get to? Is there an opportunity to advance within the company? Do you have a good place to work where your staff can grow personally, as well as in their careers? Is there mutual respect between management and employees?

He will also be likely to be happy in the job if he knows in advance exactly what the job entails and what his responsibilities are.

Is He Stable

Here you will have to look at his employment history. If he has changed jobs frequently, you cannot logically expect the pattern to change. There are dozens of good reasons for changing jobs, but be certain you understand his reasons for leaving each one. If he is taking a cut in salary to accept a job at your agency, then he might be in urgent need of income, and chances are that he will be gone as soon as he can find something offering a larger salary.

Look at his education and family background. Did he complete college, or was he a dropout? If he did leave college before he graduated, what was the reason? Has there been a recent divorce? Is he buying a home? Has he moved his place of residence frequently? Does he do any church or volunteer work? These are just some of the factors to be investigated and evaluated. There are many others which are indicative of stability (or otherwise) in a person. Get to know what they are so you can look for them in each applicant.

Can He Produce

Production can mean dollar volume of sales, or in the case of a nonselling position, it can mean a quantity of accurate work. If the applicant has produced well for previous employers, chances are that he will do so for you also. If you are filling a key sales opening, don't gamble on an unknown or unproven applicant. Always make certain the person you hire has the necessary sales experience, as well as a record of productivity in the travel field. Whatever the function of the job, the holder of it must be able to excel at it and maintain consistently high production.

You Are the Final Judge

It will be you who must make the final selection, but you cannot do so until you have complete information on each of your candidates.

Be realistic but open minded. You might well have a superior applicant when it comes to actual experience and ability, but if he is unable to work well with you and other employees, you can anticipate problems. Some people are loners—they cannot work with others and are unable to function as part of a team, but, on paper anyway, they might have the credentials you want. Here is where you will have a difficult decision to make: to either settle on this type of person or wait (hopefully) for someone else to come along who might be more conducive to teamwork.

Also remember that the references you get will only provide information to help you make the decision. The decision can only be made based upon facts and knowledge acquired during job interviews and reference checking, so evaluate each reference carefully for accuracy and objectivity. Remember to check out the references *before* you hire and not afterwards.

Look for the danger signals (red flags), and investigate each one thoroughly. You will often get an intuitive (gut) feeling about someone and this can be an important factor in your decision-making *provided* you heed it. Follow each of the hiring steps carefully, and eliminate much of the risk that inevitably goes into hiring a new employee.

6. HIRING TRAVEL SCHOOL GRADUATES

You will usually find that your training responsibilities will be considerably reduced if you hire a graduate from one of the many excellent schools which offer basic training in travel agency techniques and/or airline reservation procedures. Additionally, many colleges and junior colleges offer both credit and non-credit courses in travel and tourism, travel agency management, or something similar. (The nomenclature of travel courses varies from college to college.)

School and college graduates already know something about the basics of the travel agency business, and because of their exposure to the nuts and bolts of travel they will usually progress and learn new skills much faster than someone without such training.

There is a somewhat misguided philosophy that it is much preferable to hire someone without *any* training experience so that the manager can train the new employee "in his own way," on the theory that each manager operates differently. Such reasoning might have been acceptable a dozen or so years ago when there was a dearth of adequate travel agency training programs. Today, with the establishment of many excellent travel training schools and the introduction to travel industry training at the college and junior college levels, the wise manager will save himself a great deal of time and effort if he hires someone with such training. Virtually all private schools have placement services, and even if there is not a school in your vicinity, you should not be deterred from contacting those schools which offer residency or correspondence training, because not only might they have a recent graduate in your vicinity, but they might also know of someone who is willing to relocate for the right opportunity.

Some travel agency managers complain that the school graduates they have hired in the past "don't know anything." These managers overlook the fact that no school, no matter how broad and intensive its curriculum, is going to turn out a fully-fledged travel agent who has the ability to sit right down and go right to work without supervision or additional training. What a school *does* do is to train its students in the *basics* of tariff and ticketing, reservation procedures and many other agency functions. What you will get is someone who obviously is concerned enough about his future to invest considerable time and money in it, and someone who knows what he wants in terms of a career and possesses the basic skills. I know of a number of extremely bright school graduates who have progressed very quickly into positions of responsibility.

A school provides structured education in a controlled and protective environment. While there might be role-playing training situations, the students are not exposed to all of the pressures likely to be found in the average busy travel agency. Never assume that a school graduate is trained to the point where he can work without supervision. Look upon a good travel course as an introduction to the industry, to be supplemented by on-the-job training, tariff and ticketing sessions and fam trips.

Once you have hired a school graduate, it is essential to structure a comprehensive and ongoing training program so that the employee gradually eases into the work flow of the agency and assumes responsibility on a gradual curve. After indoctrination, you can assign your new employee to filing brochures and removing obsolete literature. If this function is handled as a part of a structured training program, it will not be the boring chore that most eager trainees would expect it to be. Up-to-date literature is the most important sales tool in any agency, and working with it on a daily basis is a fast means of learning about the many travel products on the market.

As the trainee gains confidence and knowledge, and as you gain confidence and trust in the trainee, you can assign him to do much of the simple ticketing for other counselors. He will soon progress to tickets of more complexity as well as international ticketing. Let him handle some of the airline reservations. If he is encouraged and trusted, he will soon reach the point where he can handle some of the easier transactions from beginning to conclusion. Actual progress will vary, because some people learn quicker than others, and some managers teach better than others.

Travel Training Schools

Listed below, in alphabetical order, are most of the schools which offer travel training. Some schools concentrate solely on preparing their students for the retail travel agency field, while others are extremely broad in scope and provide intensive training in a wide variety of subjects related to travel and tourism, including airline training. The graduates of these schools are ideal for your entry-level positions. Several schools offer residency, or correspondence, courses, and so draw their students from many parts of the U.S. If there is no travel school in your vicinity you could contact one of the residency training establishments as they might have a recent graduate available in your area. All schools have placement services and will be only too pleased to work with travel agents to locate suitable graduates. If you want to take an in-depth look at the curriculum of any of the schools write and ask for a current catalog. A number of colleges now offer four-year degree programs in travel and tourism. This is generally a degree in business, with a travel and tourism major. Additionally, many junior colleges offer credit programs in travel and tourism or travel agency management. There are also dozens of non-credit travel agency technique programs now being taught in the evenings in junior colleges and even in high schools. These programs are often part of adult education programs and are usually taught by a local travel agent. Because there are so many, and because of the difficulty in obtaining current information, university and college programs have been omitted. This omission should not deter you from contacting your local colleges to ascertain if they do have travel programs. You might be lucky to find an extremely competent part-time person.

Airline Schools Pacific, 6043 Hollywood Blvd., Hollywood, CA 90028
*Associated Schools, 9999 2nd Ave., Miami, FL 33138
*Braniff Education Systems, Inc., P.O. Box 35001, Dallas, TX 75235
*Briarwood School for Women, 2279 Mt. Vernon Rd., Southington, CT 06489
Carroll Travel School, Inc., 480 Central Ave., Northfield, IL 60093
Eastern School for Travel Agency Management, 721 Broadway, New York, NY 10003
Echols International Travel Training Courses, Inc., 1390 Market St., San Francisco, CA 94102
*Humboldt Institute, 2201 Blaidsell Ave., S., Minneapolis, MN 55404
International School of Travel, Inc., 21 S. 12th St., Philadelphia, PA 19107
International Travel Institute, Inc., 6401 S.W. Freeway, Houston, TX 77036
International Travel Training Courses, Inc., 936 N. Michigan Ave., Chicago, IL 60611
International Travel Training Courses, Inc., 4201 Connecticut Ave., N.W., Washington, DC 20008
*McConnel School, Inc., 1030 Nicollet Ave., Minneapolis, MN 55403
North American School of Travel, 4500 Campus Dr., Newport Beach, CA 92662 (correspondence training)
Professional Travel Agent Training School, 4501 Mission Bay Dr., San Diego, CA 92109
Roberta Fisher Travel Training School, 133 W. Wing St., Arlington Heights, IL 60005
Sobelsohn School, The, 1540 Broadway, New York, NY 10036
Travel Central, 530 Joseph Vance Bldg., Seattle, WA 98101
Travel School, The, 625 N. Michigan Ave., Chicago, IL 60611
Travel School of America, 1406 Beacon Street, Brookline, MA 02146
V.I.P. Travel Agent School, 333 E. Ontario, Chicago, IL 60611
*Wilma Boyd Career Schools, Inc., On The Plaza-Chatham Center, Pittsburgh, PA 15219

(*denotes residency training)

7. HIRING THE AGENCY MANAGER

The most important single individual in any retail travel agency is, without exception, the manager. Because the manager is so critical to efficient agency operation and growth, it is essential to employ one who can not only meet ATC and IATA requirements but who has all of the other skills associated with management functions. It is certainly necessary to be considerably more demanding and analytical of management applicants than it would be for non-management, and so locate someone who meets most of the management traits and criteria discussed elsewhere in this book.

All too many agency owners tend to hire as their manager someone who barely meets the time requirements (currently, two years' of full-time experience) of the conferences. One who meets only obligatory practical experience requirements can be considered as nothing more than a qualifier—someone who merely fulfills regulatory requirements. The guidelines which follow will be helpful when interviewing for a travel agency management position.

Travel Knowledge

The manager should be capable of compctently handling any type of business the agency is likely to generate. Apart from the run-of-the-mill transactions such as air ticketing, cruises and escorted and independent tours, the manager should be able to make sales calls, do public speaking and present travel programs to local groups, write creative sales letters, plan and implement mailings, write advertising copy, etc. The manager should also be able to sell and process group bookings, incentive travel, charter programs and similar products. Not every manager has been exposed to group-type business, but he should certainly have the ability to quickly grasp the essentials of this type of business. All too many agencies lose group business simply because no one in the agency knows how to handle it properly.

It is not usually in the best interests of the agency to have a manager bogged down with accounting and bookkeeping functions, since it is likely to detract from selling and supervisory responsibilities. But it is certainly ideal, and in many instances essential, for the manager to know how to do the ticket report and possess at least a working knowledge of travel agency accounting practices.

Supervisory Capabilities

Even in the small agency, the manager will often be required to supervise at least one other person. This means that the manager must have the ability to perform as a *manager* and be able to hire, fire, build and maintain morale, administrate and do all of the other things a manager is expected to do.

If you are an absentee owner, or a newcomer to the industry and intend to actively participate in the running of the agency yet lack the experience requirements of ATC and IATA, you would be wise to clearly define exactly who is going to be responsible for hiring, firing and general supervision of the agency. Misunderstandings often occur between owner and manager because the division of management responsibilities was not plainly and unmistakenly outlined and defined when the manager was hired.

Many owners consider the manager to be nothing more than a qualifier, and as such, they don't expect the manager to become involved with staff and other internal administrative functions of the agency. If this is what the owner intends, then a letter of agreement should be drawn up which spells out exactly those functions and responsibilities the manager can perform and those which are withheld to be handled by the owner. Such agreement should be discussed and agreed to during the interview, so that both manager and owner are fully aware of their own and each other's responsibilities.

Meeting Conference Requirements

Both ATC and IATA are quite specific in their definitions of what they mean by the term "manager," or the individual who will appear on the record as being the qualified agency manager. It is important to understand exactly what ATC and IATA demand. For example, many new agency owners have discovered that two years' full-time experience in an accredited agency is not always sufficient to qualify a new agency for accreditation.

Until quite recently, the conferences were somewhat lax in enforcing their own rules. If it could be proven that the manager had the necessary two years' of full-time experience with an accredited agency, the appointment was almost always granted, providing that all other requirements were satisfied. Such appointment is no longer automatic, and the conferences, while not demanding any more than they ever were, are now enforcing the regulations to the letter of the law rather than to the spirit of the law.

The catch is the phrase in the ATC application: "The owner, a partner, an officer or the manager of the applicant has had two years' full-time experience in *creating, generating, and promoting passenger sales and services.*" (Italics mine.)

For example, an Illinois agency was refused accreditation even though the prospective manager had no less than seven years' practical experience as a travel consultant in another agency. It turned out that during this time her *primary* responsibility was servicing commercial accounts, and as such, she lacked the two years' full-time *promotional* experience.

There have been numerous other instances where accreditation was refused because the manager failed to meet the promotional experience requirement. The conferences want to be sure that the manager not only has the ticketing and reservation procedure expertise, but also knows how to promote and generate new business.

If you are interviewing candidates for an agency management position, be certain that you thoroughly read the résumé or employment application, and carefully question your applicant to satisfy yourself that he meets all ATC and IATA regulations for managers. If in any doubt, contact a local airline sales representative or DSM, and ask for a professional opinion as to an applicant's credentials. Do it before you hire someone and not after you have filed your appointment applications. If you are refused accreditation because of inadequate experience on the part of the manager you will find it is extremely costly in terms of lost commissions, doing business without credentials, and having to start all over again and hire another manager.

Another problem area for agency management accreditation is one of possible involvement with a bankrupt agency or one which defaulted to the airlines. If your applicant has been involved in either situation, the chances are that your application will not be approved.

PART 2
Managing Your Staff

8. HOW TO TRAIN YOUR STAFF

When a new employee is hired it becomes the immediate responsibility of the agency owner or manager to get him started on the job correctly. Apart from training employees new to the industry, there should also be a continual process of training the more experienced employees. It is a mistake to assume that because someone has extensive experience he is operating efficiently. Unfortunately, many employees get into a rut, and unless there is a regular improvement program in the agency, they will tend to remain inefficient and/or unproductive.

Even if a new employee is experienced he will still require indoctrination into the way you do things in your agency. For example, your reservation card might differ slightly in format from the one to which your new employee is accustomed. You will also probably have a different way of setting up and maintaining client files, as well as different invoicing and accounting procedures.

It is not necessary to make a big production out of training. Some managers think of training as a formal affair held in a special room surrounded by books, manuals, and other devices and aids associated with training functions. While there certainly is a place for formal training, it is often more effective in the smaller agency if training is handled in a more informal and relaxed manner.

It is not difficult for a good manager to slip in and out of the training role.

Take Arlene Davis for example. She is a true professional at her job and, like any good manager, she knows her people and knows in advance where she is likely to find problems. She has six people in her office. In particular she keeps a close, though unobtrusive, eye on Joan Roberts. Arlene trained Joan for the job, and Arlene knows that Joan has not completely mastered the job. Arlene noticed that Joan was having some difficulty with an FIT routing. It was nothing of any major consequence, but it did not measure up to what Arlene expected from Joan. That afternoon Arlene stopped by

Joan's desk and said, "How's it going, Joan, are you getting that itinerary worked out o.k.?"

"Slow, but I'm getting there."

"Good, but you had better be careful with those winter train schedules because they change about the time your clients will be in Europe. Here, let's get a copy of a winter timetable and compare those schedules with summer."

For the next ten minutes, Arlene and Joan concentrated on working out the problem train schedules. Over the next few weeks Arlene dealt with each of Joan's weaknesses in very much the same way as she handled the FIT problem. Arlene knew that by using the "this-is-not-training-session" approach she was able to instill confidence and knowledge into Joan. Soon Joan was as good at her job as anyone else in the agency, thanks to Arlene's patience and informal training approach.

Know your employees, and know their weaknesses and strengths. Make a point of going through the office occasionally to see how each employee is getting along. When someone needs correcting, do it in a casual manner on the spot. Follow up (informally) within a day or two.

New employees require frequent follow-up and if you handle it informally you will soon see a gradual improvement in the employee's performance and an increase in his self-confidence.

The Trainer-Trainee Relationship

How well a trainee absorbs training will depend to a large extent upon the knowledge and ability, as well as the respect he has for the trainer.

If the trainee hasn't learned, the trainer hasn't taught.

It's true. In those cases where the trainee has failed to assimilate knowledge, it is generally because the trainee did not receive the proper instruction. It is all too easy for a manager to blame a trainee's dullness of mind, but in many failures it is the fault of the instructor who (1) lacked the ability to assume a training role, (2) did not give sufficient thought to the training curriculum, and (3) assumed the trainee could learn at a quicker pace.

Bear in mind that, to the uninitiated, the business side of travel is incredibly complex, and if you proceed too quickly your trainee will soon become confused and frustrated. Look, too, to your own ability as an instructor. Often, extremely competent and knowledgeable people are quite unable to impart their knowledge to others. They know what they want to teach, but they just don't seem to be able to get the point across. If your trainee is slower than you think he should be, look first to yourself, and be sure that the problem is not with you.

The following guidelines will help you to establish and maintain a good "teacher-pupil" relationship.

1. Reflect even temper, firmness, fairness, friendliness, patience and understanding.

2. Lead the trainee. Don't be autocratic.
3. Progress at a pace the trainee is able to maintain.
4. Maintain enthusiasm.
5. Maintain posture, neatness and poise.
6. Avoid ridicule and sarcasm.
7. Avoid profanity and vulgarity.
8. Bring in a little humor (there's a place for it) but avoid frivolity.
9. Praise good work in public, but handle poor work privately.
10. Insist on punctuality, attention and industry.
11. Follow through.

TYPES OF TRAINING

Orientation for New Employees

This is not strictly "training" but rather it is time taken out by the manager to ensure that all new employees are familiar with the policies of the agency and know what is expected of them. Even an experienced employee will feel "awkward" for the first day or two on a new job, and the manager will want to indoctrinate new employees on the first day of employment. Topics covered would be the agency policy on passes, familiarization trips, working hours, lunch and coffee breaks, vacations and holidays, and sick days. If your agency has an official policy manual (see the Appendix for a sample), it should cover just about everything your employees need to know, and it should be given to new employees on their first day of work.

Introduce the employee to the rest of the staff, and explain each employee's responsibility in the agency. Explain the literature filing system, client files, reservation procedures, and anything the employee should know about invoicing, accounting, and the ticket control systems.

On-The-Job-Training

Before you start on-the-job training, it is important to first identify exactly for what job or function you are training a person. For example, you would use a somewhat different approach and format if you were training a domestic counselor to handle international bookings than you would if you were training someone new to the industry. So first, set your overall training goal, and then establish the specific individual things a person must learn to achieve the overall goal.

Use the one-step-at-a-time method. For example, if you were training someone to sell cruises, you would want to start at the beginning:

1. Introduce the various steamship and cruise guides, including those published by the trade magazines, and cruise brochures.
2. Teach shipboard and cruising terms.
3. Explain the cabins, why one is priced higher than another, the best locations on board ship.

4. Explain the meals (first and second sitting), dress, tipping, etc.
5. Cover all shipboard activities, including shore excursions.
6. Explain the difference between ships and why some ships are better than others.
7. Show the trainee how to complete a reservation request.
8. Explain how to discuss cruising with the client. Let your trainee sit in on counselor-client discussions.

This is perhaps a somewhat simplified training format, but it will serve to illustrate how to start with the basics and work up on a step-by-step basis to the more complex features of cruising.

As soon as the trainee has mastered one step, go on to the next, but make a habit of returning to review each topic previously covered to ensure that the trainee has mastered it.

1. Cover one function at a time.
2. Review the trainee's work, and ensure that training assignments are being carried out properly.
3. Test your trainee by giving a written assignment at each stage. For example, if you are teaching domestic ticketing, let the trainee work out itineraries using the OAG. Progress from relatively simple routings to those of more complexity.
4. Frankly discuss progress emphasizing the importance of proper work habits.
5. Set part of each training session aside to discuss previous sessions. Ask your trainee to summarize what he learned in previous meetings.

Training Meetings

Regularly scheduled training meetings are an excellent means of developing the skills of all travel agency employees. Instruction sessions don't have to consist of a discourse by the manager, and will be far more effective if they are structured in such a way that there is adequate room for discussion and a free flow of ideas.

Remember that *any* meeting is an investment in time—both for the leader and the participants, so it is important to structure training sessions in such a way that they fulfill their objective in as little time as possible. Long, drawn out meetings soon become tedious and people will soon lose interest and become bored. A monotonous meeting will not accomplish the intended goal and will waste everyone's time.

1. Know your objective and put it down on paper.
2. Prepare your meeting. Decide if it will be at your desk, in the office, or in a meeting room. Decide what aids you need. Will you use a blackboard, handouts, etc.? Whatever you do use should be prepared ahead of time.
3. Prepare your employees by announcing the meeting ahead of time. Give the participants at least a day to think about the agenda.

4. Set a time limit and let your employees know what it is.
5. Start your meeting on time. Start by telling your staff the objective of the meeting. Many good meetings fail simply because the trainer failed to communicate the objective.
6. Follow your outline, because if you don't, you won't be able to accomplish your purpose within your time limit.
7. Allow time for questions and discussion.
8. Control the meeting. Bring discussion back on track if it wanders. Make every minute count.
9. Finish promptly. Your meeting must be decisive to be successful. Bring it to a firm, prompt conclusion.
10. Follow up.

Role-Playing

Role-playing can be extremely productive and instructional to everyone involved. While some people might tend to be self-conscious in the beginning, they will soon enter into the spirit of the thing.

If your staff are not used to role-playing situations, introduce them to it gradually by selecting the "players" in advance. Let them prepare themselves so that when acting out or simulating client-customer situations they will feel comfortable doing so. When the employees become used to role-playing you can then assign roles at the start of the meeting so that you can see how they perform without advance notice. Make certain that everyone has the opportunity to play all roles. At the conclusion of the practice the leader should review it and hold a discussion on what took place. Let other employees comment and perhaps give examples of how they would handle similar situations.

Familiarization Trips

The sole purpose of familiarization trips is one of education. Fam trips are not supposed to be junkets (though many are treated as such), but are intended to introduce the travel agent to an area he has not previously visited or to a product with which he is unfamiliar.

Encourage fam trips for everyone in your agency. Fam trips should be part of every employee's training and development, and they are a splendid means of improving knowledge at little or no cost to the agency. If each employee participates in at least one fam trip a year, the agency will soon become known and recognized for its professional, competent and knowledgeable staff.

Treat all fam trips as educational ventures by requesting the employee to prepare a written report. It is also a good idea to have the employee report to the entire staff so that fam trips can be used as a training experience for everyone and not just the participant.

I once met a manager who always carried a small, battery-operated cassette tape recorder with her so that she could record her experiences and opinions while they were still fresh in her mind. When she returned to her office she called a meeting of her staff, played the cassettes, and answered questions about the area. She also made her recorder available to each employee when they went on a fam trip. Needless to say, her agency was one of the most efficient, and had the best-trained staff in the community. This manager recognized fam trips as an extremely valuable method of training her employees.

Structured Training

More and more emphasis has been placed on structured travel industry training during the last decade or so. There is now a wide range of excellent training programs, which range from the relatively basic ASTA Correspondence Course, up to the management courses offered at Breech Training Academy, and the certification program of the Institute of Certified Travel Agents (ICTA). There is something for virtually everyone—from beginner to agency manager and owner.

The only unfortunate thing about these training programs is that all too few people take advantage of them. For example, many managers and owners tend to be somewhat complacent, and scorn anything which requires study, or instruction in an educational environment. "Oh, we don't need that stuff," they'll say. "We've been selling travel for years and there's nothing we can learn in a classroom."

Such thinking might have been acceptable fifteen or twenty years ago, but the travel industry has changed drastically in that time. Competition is greater, travel trends have changed, and the modern traveler is certainly more sophisticated than was his counterpart of a few years ago. The travel agency manager of today must know far more than being able to put an FIT together or construct an air fare.

The travel agency business has grown phenomenally in twenty years, yet the number of well-trained staff has not kept pace with the growth of the industry. As every manager knows, it has become extremely difficult to find top-notch employees. As every owner is aware, it is also next to impossible to find managers with the necessary credentials to run an agency. There are many people running agencies who may have adequate travel knowledge but who lack the experience and skills to properly manage an agency from the business perspective.

The call for increased professionalism in the travel agency business is growing each year. Also, the very competitiveness of the industry requires greater business expertise and management ability. If you are unwilling to consider some of the management improvement courses available to you, you are likely to be left behind as the travel business attracts more and more people who, while they might lack immediate travel knowledge, do possess a high degree of business acumen and aggressive marketing techniques.

Many newcomers to the field are bringing sophisticated and proven business methods with them and applying them to travel. Most of them have been tremendously successful, and have quickly built up enormously successful and profitable agencies.

One reason that many larger corporations are so successful is because both management and non-management staff are required to attend training and upgrading sessions each year. Many millions of dollars are spent by American corporations on teaching managers how to be better managers, and instructing other employees how to perform their jobs better.

Because of the individualistic nature of the travel agency business, it must be up to each manager and each owner to first recognize that self-improvement is essential to growth and perhaps even the survival of their agency, and then embark upon a structured program to upgrade their management skills and business techniques. Almost everyone sets time aside each year for vacations and fam trips, but few are willing to allot the same period of time to taking a management course or for working towards a CTC diploma.

Participation in structured training takes time and money, but the end result means better management, and higher quality, more professional and more productive employees. It also means more successful and more profitable travel agencies.

Training Programs and Training Aids

Airline Ticketing and Training Seminars

These are conducted by the airlines at regular intervals in most major cities. Instruction is given in both domestic and international tariff and ticketing at basic, intermediate and advanced levels. Contact your local airline sales representatives for information on seminars in your area.

Air Traffic Conference Travel Agency Training Program
6151 W. Century Blvd.
Los Angeles, CA 90045

Offers two five-day courses. Air Travel Planning I is designed to provide basic and refresher ticketing and tariff training. Air Travel Planning II specializes in the more complex application of tariff and ticketing, with special emphasis on promotional fares. Write for brochure of dates and costs.

American Society of Travel Agents
711 Fifth Avenue
New York, NY 10022

ASTA offers a number of training programs, the more important of which are listed here. Contact ASTA for more detailed information on these and other ASTA training material.

ASTA Travel Correspondence Course

Covers the basic skills of the travel agency business and is an ideal program for the employee new to the industry.

ASTA School at Sea

Conducted in co-operation with various steamship and cruise lines. Shipboard instruction covers all subjects relative to cruise and steamship travel.

Association of Retail Travel Agents
8 Maple Street
Croton-on-Hudson, NY 10520

Sponsors a series of weekend seminars at TWA's Breech Training Academy in Kansas City. One program is conducted for owners and managers and another for counselors, group organizers and outside sales representatives. Write ARTA for current schedules.

Breech Training Academy
6300 Lamar Avenue
Overland Park, KS 66201

Breech Training Academy, operated by Trans World Airlines, offers a number of in-depth training programs suitable for travel agency owners and managers as well as selling staff. Courses include Product Knowledge I and Product Knowledge II; Agency Sales and Marketing Development; Travel Agency Management; Air Tariff (International); and, Agency Automated Training. These are all five-day courses conducted in an academic atmosphere. They are highly recommended as a means of improving knowledge, skills and management techniques. Write for brochure which contains detailed information and costs.

Institute of Certified Travel Agents
P.O. Box 56
Wellesley, MA 02181

The study program offered by ICTA leads directly to the Certified Travel Counselor (CTC) accreditation. This is an extremely comprehensive program, but when completed, the CTC initials after your name indicate to others in the travel industry, as well as to the general public, that you have achieved an advanced level of professional training. Contact ICTA for complete information on their programs.

Other Training Materials

Travel Marketing and Agency Management Guidelines

This bi-monthly management publication, edited by Armin D. Lehmann, covers such topics as salesmanship, travel agency marketing ideas, advertising tips, how to sell groups, tour operating advice, etc. It is packed with valuable information to help the agency owner or manager run a profitable, efficient and professional agency. An extremely valuable management tool and well worth the $20 annual subscription. Order from Travel Marketing, 309 Santa Monica Blvd., Santa Monica, CA 90401

Travel and Tourism: An Introduction to Travel Agency Operations

This comprehensive, 360-page textbook by Armin D. Lehmann is completely illustrated, and an up-to-date guide for all travel agency personnel. It is especially useful as a training aid for introducing new employees to the travel agency business. $18.50 includes postage. Order from Travel Marketing, 309 Santa Monica Blvd., Santa Monica, CA 90401

OAG Instruction

Two helpful publications for training new employees and introducing them to the OAG are *Initial Instruction in the Use of International Edition, Official Airline Guide,* and *Initial Instruction in the Use of the North American Edition, Official Airline Guide.* Available from Reuben H. Donnelley Corporation, 2000 Clearwater Drive, Oak Brook, IL 60521.

The ABCs of Travel

A glossary of terms and abbreviations peculiar to the travel industry. An ideal publication to introduce your new employees to the language of travel. $2 from Travel Weekly, One Park Avenue, New York, NY 10016

9. HOW TO COMPENSATE YOUR STAFF

When preparing an employee compensation program, take into consideration the complete range of benefits available to travel staff, and plan, and be prepared to offer, a total package rather than just a basic salary. Today, people demand far more from life than the three fundamental needs of food, clothing and shelter, and modern employees are far more conscious of fringe benefits than were their counterparts of a generation ago. Most job-hunters will diligently seek out an employer who offers a comprehensive range of benefits, and unless you have a balanced compensation package you can expect to lose staff to those agencies which do offer a broad range of benefits.

Not every agency can offer everything listed in this section, but you can at least review your own policies and compare them with the benefits now being offered to travel staff. If you cannot incorporate a benefit just as it is described, remember that these are only examples, so feel free to adapt them to your own particular situation.

You should also bear in mind that the better and more complete your total compensation package, the easier it will be for you to not only attract top quality staff to your agency, but to keep them once you have them.

A comprehensive range of available benefits would include:

1. An adequate salary.
2. A merit salary review at least once each year.
3. A cost of living review as required.
4. Profit sharing and/or incentive programs.
5. Medical and life insurance coverage.
6. The availability of familiarization trips.
7. ATC and IATA passes.
8. An equitable vacation policy.
9. A pre-determined number of paid sick days.
10. A retirement program.

An Adequate Salary

There is a wide disparity when it comes to salaries in the travel agency field, and there is considerable variance not only between city and suburbs, but even within the same community. When you determine salary levels, you cannot, if you expect to keep your staff, underpay them. If you do, you are likely to encounter an unusually high turnover of staff which is an expensive proposition in any agency, but even more so in a small one.

If you lean too far the other way and tend to overpay your employees, you will perhaps strain your budget and operating expenses beyond their capacity, or even dangerously deplete your cash and the earnings of the agency.

Try to arrive at a fair salary *range* for each position in the agency, and be sure to base it on the *average* for your area. Perhaps the best rule of thumb is to pay your staff as well as you can afford to, providing your salaries are within the range for your area. It is also a good idea to allow some degree of flexibility. For example, if you have established that you want to pay a maximum starting salary of $700 a month, but you have an applicant who is obviously above average but who will consider nothing less than $750, what do you do?

If you are convinced that the applicant can do a superior job for you and can generate and service substantial business, then $50 is of no real consequence. The point is not to allow yourself to be locked into a set pattern or budget. Be prepared to pay above the norm when you have to, or when you have the opportunity to hire a superior employee.

Merit Salary Reviews

Review salaries at least once each year, and even twice if the salary is below average for the job. Just because you review an employee's salary should not guarantee him an automatic increase; raises should be based upon merit and related directly to job performance. If you hired a new employee at a low salary, it is a good idea to review it after three to six months on the job, and relate your increases to how well the employee is learning the business and assimilating new skills.

Cost of Living Reviews

Everyone is caught up in the inflation spiral, so you might want to consider giving an across-the-board increase to everyone on your payroll. Since this type of increase is not tied to job performance, it should be based upon a percentage figure—e.g. 3 percent of current salary.

Profit-Sharing and Incentive Programs

There are several methods of implementing these plans in a retail travel agency. For more in-depth information and suggested programs, refer to Chapter 10.

Medical and Life Insurance Premiums

More and more small employers, including travel agencies, are now assuming the cost of either all or part of medical insurance premiums for their employees. Some larger agencies also have life insurance programs available. Company-paid medical premiums are becoming more and more important, and many employees seek out those agencies which offer paid medical programs.

Familiarization Trips

Fam trips are an important, if not an essential, benefit of the travel agency profession. The salary of the average travel agency employee is often below that of those employed in other fields; therefore, compensation must be made to employees in other ways, such as fam trips and reduced-rate travel privileges. Fam trips, if they are used for the purpose for which they are intended, offer a splendid means to improve the knowledge and skills of the agency staff at little or no cost to the agency.

The policy of familiarization trips should be governed by the size of the agency, but as a rule of thumb, try to allot at least one fam trip each year to each qualified employee. Try to send employees on trips to areas they have never previously visited, so that they gain additional knowledge and practical experience, which in turn, will result in their being more skilled and professional in the agency.

Some agency owners withhold an employee's salary when the employee is participating in a fam trip. It hardly seems fair to penalize someone for taking advantage of a benefit of the industry, and who is going to be of more value to the agency upon return to the office. These owners are also laying the groundwork for possible salary claims in the event the employee leaves the agency. Fam trips are considered to be educational in nature, so it is quite possible for an employee to claim not only his full salary while away on such a trip but also possible overtime at time and a half for all hours over 40 spent working on such a trip.

A more considerate, and therefore a more successful, agency owner will not only pay the employee his normal salary but will also assume the cost of the fam trip itself.

ATC and IATA Passes

This is another area where unqualified owners have been known to use all of the ATC and IATA passes, and the eligible employees are passed over. Reduced-rate travel is a necessary benefit for those who work in a travel agency. The fairest way to distribute ATC and IATA passes is to ensure that each employee is alloted one of each per year. One pass could be tied to a fam trip, and the other could be used for vacation purposes to any destination of the employee's choice.

Vacation Policies and Paid Holidays

A good rule of thumb is to give your employees two weeks' paid vacation after one year of employment. You might want to make an employee eligible for one week after he has worked for six full months. After five years of service give three weeks vacation and after ten years, one calendar month. Here again, there are no norms, and some agencies give three weeks after three years of service and one month after five years.

Paid holidays include such days as Christmas, New Years Day, Memorial Day, Independence Day, Labor Day and Thanksgiving.

Paid Sick Days

Health problems are unavoidable, so allow your employees a set number of days each year when they will be paid if they are unable to report to work for medical reasons. Again, there are no norms, as some agencies allow sick days to accrue from the first day of employment, while others insist that an employee be on the payroll for at least six months before becoming eligible. Five or six days a year would be quite adequate. Employees should not be allowed to carry over unused sick days from one year to another.

Retirement Program

Such a program is rare in most small travel agencies, and few employees participate in retirement programs unless they happen to work for one of the larger travel companies. However, if an owner has not established a retirement program, he should certainly investigate one where he can set aside retirement dollars into an approved IRA plan. Such contributions can result in a reduction of current tax obligations, since they are not taxed at the current rate, and will not be taxed until retirement, when they will be taxed at a lower rate.

Pension plans are well worth investigating. You can set one up for yourself (Individual Retirement Account), or establish a corporate plan. You could also set up a plan which will allow the employees to make their own contributions.

As you review your overall benefits and personnel policies, try to include as many as you can, commensurate of course with the size and with the earnings of your agency.

10. INCENTIVE AND PROFIT-SHARING PROGRAMS

The dictionary tells us that the word "incentive" means to motivate, to stimulate to action, or the offering of an inducement by a business firm to promote sales, productivity, or extra effort by personnel.

Incentive and profit-sharing programs, if set up properly and administered fairly, are useful in motivating both agency management and sales staff and provide them with the opportunity to relate their income directly to either their own sales and production or to the total sales or profits of the agency. If there is a lazy counselor on the staff, a good incentive or profit-sharing plan will either inspire him to higher production or will encourage him to seek a safer position elsewhere.

It is important to note that the examples described should not be considered rigid. They are only suggestions and samples of feasible programs which can be used as-is or converted and adapted to a specific agency or situation.

It is also important to remember that the specific purpose of any incentive or profit-sharing program is to increase business, and thereby improve the profitability of the agency. All programs should, therefore, be challenging; at the same time, they must be achievable with extra effort on the part of the employees.

Vesting

Tenure with the agency should also be an important factor, and the management will have to determine the length of time an employee must be with the agency in order to be eligible for participation in the company incentive and/or profit-sharing program. While an incentive plan need not require the tenure of a profit-sharing plan, it is wise to establish a minimum period. When it comes to profit sharing, many agencies require thirty-six months' of full-time, continuous employment with the agency before an employee is vested. Other agencies set the time period to twenty-four months or even one year. Participation should, in general, be extended only to full-time salaried employees. Part-timers and commissioned sales persons should be excluded.

Budgeting

Before introducing any profit-sharing or incentive plan, it is important to review the annual budget and sales figures of the agency. The previous year's sales figures and profits should be carefully compared with those budgeted for the forthcoming year. The agency mix, operating expenses, and other related factors must also be reviewed. The owner must also determine in advance just what the overall goal is, what achievements are to be expected, and if the agency can afford to implement such programs. Once an announcement has been made to the staff, it is practically impossible to cancel such plans without incurring ill-will or even hostility on the part of the employees.

INCENTIVE PROGRAMS

A new, or a marginally profitable, agency often cannot afford to support a profit-sharing plan for the simple reason that there are no profits to distribute, or the agency is hard-pressed for cash—a somewhat scarce commodity in many smaller agencies. But such an agency can and should be prepared to implement some type of incentive program.

It is important to note that *incentive* and *profit sharing* are two entirely different things. An *incentive* is an inducement while *profit sharing* is related directly to the profits of the agency, after all salaries and operating expenses have been deducted from commissions.

An incentive plan need not be as ambitious as a profit-sharing program, but it should at least be structured in such a way that the participants do feel that it is worth their while to take the time and make the effort to accomplish the goal. An incentive plan frequently can be instrumental in boosting sales of the new agency, and so provide it with somewhat faster growth than it might have enjoyed without such a program.

Incentives should, by no means, be confined to new and small agencies; they are suitable for implementation in any agency, because they are relatively simple to administer, and they can be tied to the sales of the agency or to the sales of the individual.

The actual stimuli need not be of great expense to the agency in terms of actual cash outlay. Examples might include an additional week of vacation with pay, an extra familiarization trip, a cruise, or perhaps a domestic or international tour package. If the employee is qualified under ATC and IATA rules, then an air ticket could be offered to some pre-established domestic or foreign destination.

PROFIT-SHARING PLANS

A profit-sharing plan is one which is related to the net profit of the agency. Profit sharing can also be defined as that portion or percentage of the agency earnings the management or ownership chooses to share among its employees. It is unnecessary to inform employees exactly what the profit is in terms of dollars and cents, but many owners do let their staff know the amount of cash available for distribution.

A profit-sharing plan must also be contingent on the fact that the earnings are sufficient to enable management to designate a portion of them to the program. Profit sharing also rewards the employees for their contribution in good years, and penalizes them in those years when sales are below par.

Examples of Profit-Sharing Plans

There are several methods and mathematical formulas suitable for administering profit-sharing programs. There are also inequities in each of them. The plan which probably is the fairest to all concerned is one which is based on tenure with the agency.

In the following examples, the hypothetical agency earned a net profit of $25,000, and 10 percent, or $2,500 is to be divided among the five employees.

Plan I is based on the employee's value and contribution to the agency sales, commissions and profits of the agency. In this example, an international counselor was considered by management to be the most valuable contributor and was alloted five points, while the typist received only one point. The vesting period is twenty-four months' continuous employment.

Plan II is based solely on tenure, and position in the agency is not a consideration.

PROFIT-SHARING PLAN I

Available for distribution $2,500
Vesting period 24 months

Step 1. Allot point to each eligible employee based on the employee's contribution to sales and profits.
Step 2. Add the total number of points alloted (17 in this example).
Step 3. Divide the total to be distributed ($2,500) by the number of points alloted (17). The result ($147.06) becomes the point factor.
Step. 4. Multiply the number of points alloted to each employee by the point factor ($147.06).

Example:

International counselor	5 pts.	($147.06 each)	$ 735.30
Domestic counselor	4 pts.	($147.06 each)	$ 588.24
Domestic counselor	4 pts.	($147.06 each)	$ 588.24
Ticketing clerk	3 pts.	($147.06 each)	$ 441.18
Typist	1 pt.	($147.06 each)	$ 147.06
Totals	17 pts.		$2,500.02

PROFIT-SHARING PLAN II

Available for distribution $2,500
Vesting period 24 months

Step 1. a. Allot one point for the vesting period; b. For each additional calendar month in excess of 24 months, add one additional point.
Step 2. Add the total number of points (73).
Step 3. Divide the total to be distributed ($2,500) by the total number of points (73), thereby resulting in 34.25. The point factor in this case is $34.25.
Step 4. Multiply the number of points allotted to each employee by the point factor (34.25).

Example:
For two years' minimum service:		1 point
For each calendar month in excess of two years:		1 point
International counselor	3 yrs 2 mos. X 15 pts. =	$ 513.75
Domestic counselor	5 yrs 1 mo. X 38 pts. =	$1,301.50
Domestic counselor	3 yrs 1 mo. X 14 pts. =	$ 479.50
Ticketing clerk	2 yrs 3 mos. X 4 pts. =	$ 137.00
Typist	2 yrs 1 mo. X 2 pts. =	$ 68.50
Totals	73 pts.	$2,500.25

11. WAGE AND HOUR LAWS. DISCRIMINATION

The Fair Labor Standards Act

This Act establishes the minimum wage, overtime pay, equal pay and child labor standards. Additionally, almost every state has enacted its own wage and hour laws which are often stricter than those of the federal government. In those states where state laws are more stringent than federal, the state laws take precedence. Because each state is different, it is impossible to include even a sampling of state wage and hour laws here, and only federal standards will be covered; they will serve as guidelines and alert you to the basics of some of the laws which will influence your business. However, to avoid possible prosecution, it is suggested that if you have not already done so, you familiarize yourself with the wage and hour laws of your own state.

As the Federal Act relates to a travel agency, all agencies with an annual gross sales volume of not less than $275,000 are subject to the Act and must pay their employees the minimum wage of $2.90 an hour. As of January 1980, the minimum hourly wage will be $3.10 and as of January 1, 1981 the minimum hourly wage will increase to $3.35.

Exemptions

Some employees are exempt from the minimum wage and/or overtime provisions. Such exemptions might (but not always) include agency managers and commissions sales staff.

It should also be noted that a title does not necessarily exempt someone from overtime pay eligibility. For example, in the travel agency business, it is necessary to employ a "manager" with specific credentials in order to qualify the agency for ATC and IATA appointments. Often, such a person is manager in name only and is hired to meet obligatory requirements, while the agency owner performs all actual management and supervisory functions. In such a case, the manager would not be considered to be an exempt employee and would, in all probability, be entitled to overtime compensation.

In order for an employee to be exempt as a bona fide executive, all of the following tests must be met:

1. The employee's primary duty must be management of the agency, or in the case of a larger company, of a recognized department or division.
2. The employee must customarily and regularly direct the work of at least two or more other employees.
3. The employee must have the authority to hire or fire, or be able to recommend hiring and firing.
4. The employee must customarily and regularly exercise discretionary powers.
5. The employee must devote no more than 20 percent (less than 40 percent if employed by a retail or service establishment) of his hours worked to activities not directly and closely related to the managerial duties.
6. The employee must be paid on a salary basis at the rate of at least $155 a week.

Overtime

Overtime must be paid at a rate of at least one and one half times the employee's regular pay rate for each hour worked in a workweek of forty hours. It is important to remember that each workweek stands alone, and there can be no averaging of two or more workweeks. If time off is given in lieu of overtime pay, then it must be given in the same pay week. Compensating time off must be at the employee's election, and it must be given during a period when the employee would normally be working. An example of this might be if an employee were required to remain for an hour one evening to complete air tickets, or other documentation, then he could *elect* to either come to the office one hour later or leave one hour earlier on a day during the same workweek, or he could elect to claim overtime at time and a half.

Familiarization Trip and Other Compensation

The intention of fam trips is one of education, rather than one of junketing. If an employee is *requested* by the agency owner or manager to participate in a fam trip with the understanding that such participation is intended to be a learning experience, and is a requirement of the job, then the employee would be well within his rights to claim overtime compensation for all extra hours spent working on such a trip.

To protect the agency against possible future claims of unpaid overtime, the wise agency owner or manager will insist on a formal letter of agreement with all agency employees participating in fam trips. Such a letter should clearly state that (1) the employee is participating in such a trip voluntarily and not at the request of the employer; and, (2) all hours over forty in any one workweek are to be considered as the employee's own to do with as he pleases.

It is also customary in the travel agency business to attend evening cocktail parties, receptions, sales presentations and dinners. It will, perhaps, come as a shock to many agency owners and managers to learn that employees who attend such functions are entitled to overtime or compensating time off *if* they are requested or required to attend such travel industry functions.

Again, the agency can be protected against possible claims by disgruntled employees if it is made clear (in writing) that it is agency policy to encourage attendance at such functions, but attendance is not mandatory, and that no overtime will be paid nor compensating time off be given.

Record Keeping

To comply with the Act, and to refute possible future overtime claims, it is necessary to maintain accurate records for each employee. There are many "standard" time record sheets available at office supply and stationery stores which meet compliance with both state and federal laws. The agency owner or manager should ensure that all employees sign their arrival and departure times each day. These time sheets should be considered as valuable records, and as such, should be stored in a safe place.

Equal Opportunity

The Civil Rights Act of 1964 states that no one can be denied a job, or fair treatment in that job, because of discrimination on account of race, color, religion, sex or national origin. The Act is supervised and enforced by the U.S. Equal Employment and Opportunity Commission (EEOC).

Basically, an employer cannot discriminate in any way with regard to classified advertising, hiring or firing, different wages for equal work, and several other areas.

For example, if you have a job opening for a domestic consultant and specifically want a female in the position, you cannot run a classified Help Wanted advertisement stating that you want a female. All newspapers and trade magazines which accept this type of classified advertising are aware of the law, and will not accept any ad which violates the law or is discriminatory.

There are other areas that require caution on the part of employers. For instance, you can only judge job applicants on their experience and qualifications for the job. If you have always had a man in the position, and a female applies, she must be considered equally with male applicants. An illustration of this would be a sales representative position (traditionally a man's job), for which a woman applies. She must, under the law, be considered equally with males. You cannot use excuses such as it's a man's job, or there is too much traveling, or the roads are unsafe for female drivers (especially if the car breaks down), or there is lifting of heavy boxes of brochures, or other such double standards.

In the employment application, or during the interview, you cannot ask separate questions of men and women. For example, you cannot ask a woman what arrangements she has made to take care of her small children while she is working *unless* you are prepared to ask the same question of male applicants. You cannot ask a woman if she is pregnant, or if she is planning to have a family. There are many other questions and areas, which, if brought up, violate the law.

Further Study

There are a number of helpful booklets available which cover wage and hour laws in more depth. The following are free and are available from the U.S. Department of Labor, Employment Standards Administration, Wage and Hour Division.

Handy Reference Guide to the Fair Labor Standards Act
(WH publication 1282)
Hours Worked Under the Fair Labor Standards Act
(WH publication 1344)
Executive, Administrative, Professional and Outside Salesmen Exemptions Under the Fair Labor Standards Act
(WH publication 1363)

12. HOW TO BUILD AND MAINTAIN MORALE

Throughout history, the great leaders of men have known that the success of any enterprise, and the ability to accomplish their goals, were contingent upon the morale of their followers.

The morale and output of employees is dependent upon the leadership qualities of the supervisor or manager.

Never forget this, because it applies to all offices and to all organizations, large and small. If morale is low, it almost always follows that this condition has been brought about by management. (A weak manager will tend to blame his staff for low morale rather than look to how he is functioning as a manager.) Never underestimate the power of morale in your office. And never forget that good morale will contribute substantially to the success and growth of your agency, while poor morale can quickly and surely destroy you.

The dictionary defines morale as a moral or mental condition as regards to courage, zeal, confidence, discipline and enthusiasm. In business, morale is described as being high or low, good or bad. Because high morale is so essential to the success of almost any business, the manager must make every effort to ensure that employee morale is maintained at its highest level.

When morale is good, the employees reflect their satisfaction by good attendance, punctuality, an abundance of accurate work, high sales, good telephone manners, long hours, and smiling, friendly faces. The relationship between the manager and the staff is easy and relaxed, with trust and a mutual respect.

Conversely, low morale can be detected by absenteeism, tardiness, low sales, below average output of work, client complaints, bad telephone manners, surliness, costly errors, petty squabbling, and a general air of gloom and negativity in the agency.

Know Thyself

What type of a supervisor are you? Self-evaluation is not easy for most of us; we have to contend with our own egos, and we almost never see ourselves as others—especially our subordinates—see us. If you already have the knack of handling people, that is splendid. But if you do not have the ability, it can be acquired if you are receptive to learning new skills and engaging in some down-to-earth self-evaluation. Each one of us can probably improve our ability to lead others—not all of us are born leaders: we must acquire the art as we go through life.

Before we can progress even the slightest distance, we must first recognize exactly where our weaknesses are. If we are aware of our failings, we are well on our way to becoming leaders, and we will quickly assimilate the knowledge and skills required to effectively build and maintain good morale in our employees.

Apart from the "middle-of-the-road-make-no-waves" type of manager, there are really only two distinct methods of supervision. After you have studied these management categories, you will be able to place yourself in one of them.

High Morale Managers

They practice the modern, democratic method of management, and recognize that their personal success, as well as the growth and efficiency of the business, is determined to a large extent upon the morale of their staff. They look upon those whom they supervise as equals and appreciate their opinions and suggestions. They encourage initiative in their staff because it leads to additional responsibilities, achievements and job satisfaction. They have a strong sense of security in their job and within themselves, and they instill this feeling into their employees. They always let their employees know where they stand as it relates to their work and job performance. They like people, and they enjoy taking a strong interest in them. They have a genuine concern for the problems of their employees, and they assist their subordinates in every way they can. They praise their employees more than they criticize them. They are excellent judges of people, and are skilled at handling them.

Low Morale Managers

Most of the time they carry out their supervisory responsibilities in an autocratic manner, and they place their staff under pressure. They cannot delegate responsibility and must almost always "do it themselves." They never have the time or the inclination to listen to what their staff have to say, and never discuss the problems of those who work for them. They *tell* their staff what to do and never *ask* them. They talk down to their employees and are quick to temper. Their staff meetings are speeches, rather than a democratic forum of ideas. Their offices experience above average turnover of staff. They never tell their staff what is going on. The staff are generally unhappy, and there is constant friction and petty bickering in the office.

What You Can Do to Build Morale

You have just read about two entirely different types of manager, and if this prompts you to want to change your management techniques, you should make immediate plans to do so. Morale cannot be changed overnight; it takes a plan of slow growth and needs nurturing over a period of weeks—even months. Creating good morale in your subordinates must be accomplished by design, consciously, and not by haphazard planning. The result of months, or even years, of effort to establish high morale can be changed overnight by insignificant events sometimes difficult to pinpoint.

Be a Better Supervisor

Take the time to really understand those whom you supervise. Treat them with courtesy, respect and consideration. When things go wrong for them, help them solve the problem. Lead them. People who are followers *want* to be led. They need leadership from someone whom they can look up to and respect.

What Employees Want Most in a Job

If you know what employees expect most in their work environment, you are well on your way to building good morale. There are four major factors to consider in the needs of employees:

1. Job security
2. Opportunity for advancement
3. A good and fair salary
4. Other (fringe) benefits

Your Checklist for Building Morale

Here is a list of the major policies you should implement in order to build and maintain good morale in your office.

1. Publicly appreciate, recognize and praise good work and ideas.
2. If you must criticize or discipline, do it in private.
3. Make the staff feel important by asking for their ideas and views. Discuss policy changes prior to implementation, and give employees the time they need when they come to you. Leave your door open and encourage them to consult you as an equal. Remember, their ideas and suggestions are free, and they just might be better than your own.
4. Pay your staff fairly for the work performed, and review at least once each year. Consider cost of living increases.
5. Let the staff know where they stand at all times.
6. Within your budget and financial capabilities provide as many fringe benefits as you can. (Insurance, bonus, vacations, etc.).
7. Make certain that each employee is in the right job. Let him know where he fits in the overall picture.
8. Provide good working conditions. Only you can set the environment in which your staff work; you can make it pleasant or unpleasant. It is to your advantage to keep the staff happy.
9. Promote from within whenever possible. Encourage the staff to learn new skills, to advance, and to accept responsibility.
10. Let your staff know they are secure in their jobs.

GOOD MANAGEMENT IS GETTING THINGS DONE THROUGH PEOPLE

13. EVALUATING EMPLOYEE PERFORMANCE

Sooner or later every employee will want to know:

What is expected of me?
How am I doing?
Where do I stand?
How can I improve?

It is essential to evaluate your employees at least once, and sometimes twice, each year. An annual review of performance is invaluable in approving equitable salary increases, as well as ascertaining potential for promotion and the ability to assume greater responsibility. You will also have a permanent record of job performance should a new manager come along and inherit your staff, or should another employer require a reference.

To be able to measure job performance correctly, it is necessary to consider ten important factors:

1. Knowledge of the job
2. Quantity of work
3. Quality of work
4. Cooperation

EMPLOYEE'S PERFORMANCE RATING FORMULA

Here is a simple evaluation format which will allow you to appraise performance of your staff accurately. The employee will be evaluated on five important criteria and rated on his performance in each *category*. The *quality* or *standard* of performance carries a numerical value from 10 (poor) to 50 (excellent). After you have carefully and objectively rated in each classification, total the complete numerical values and then divide this number by five to arrive at the standard of performance.

Quality rating:	poor	satis-factory	good	very good	excel-lent	numerical value
Numerical value:	10	20	30	40	50	
Extent of knowledge		X				20
Volume of work			X			30
Accuracy and thoroughness		X				20
Ability to work with others	X					10
Supervision required			X			30

total value: 110
Divide the total value by five = 22*

Use chart below to arrive at overall evaluation.

10.00 to 15.00 = poor
15.10 to 25.00 = satisfactory
25.10 to 35.00 = good
35.10 to 45.00 = very good
45.10 to 50.00 = excellent

* In this example, the employee would be evaluated overall as "satisfactory."

5. Personality
6. Dependability
7. Judgment
8. Attendance
9. Potential
10. Punctuality

These factors are common in most types of work, and to apply them accurately to an individual and arrive at a fair and a total evaluation, you must appraise the employee on each one separately.

As you prepare the evaluation consider each factor carefully, and do not allow one trait or fault to influence the entire appraisal. For example, an employee might possess tremendous knowledge of the job, but his output of work is below average. In such a case, you would then rate him high on knowledge but low on quantity, and would then consider each of the other factors until you arrived at the final evaluation.

Do not base your ratings on impressions—only on known facts. Never let length of service influence your decision, since a counselor who has been in your employ for one year might contribute substantially greater sales and earnings than someone who has been around for five years.

Above all, *never* let your personal feelings enter into an evaluation. An employee should be judged on his performance on the job, and not on whether or not you like him as a person. There is a tendency for us to attribute greater efficiency to those whom we like personally. In all fairness, you must be objective when you evaluate.

There are five performance grades in which to place an employee:

1. Poor—(Found in about five percent of an employee group).
2. Satisfactory—(Found in about fifteen percent of an employee group).
3. Average—(Expected of most employees. About fifty percent fall into this category).
4. Very good—(Found in about twenty percent of an employee group.)
5. Excellent—(Well above average. Found in about ten percent of employees).

Discuss Your Evaluation With Employee

An evaluation is worthless unless the results can be put to constructive use. Most employees *want* to know how they are performing—especially if they are ambitious—and this requires a discussion of the evaluation with the employee. A frank and open discussion will improve your relationship with your subordinates.

Plan the evaluation meeting very carefully, and try to hold it in a location where you will not be interrupted by telephone calls and clients. Put the employee at ease by first going over his assets and good qualities. Let him know where he excels and that you appreciate all of his good points. To be completely objective, you must clearly identify those areas which require improvement. Here you must be careful to be constructive rather than overly critical, because if you place the employee in a position where he feels inferior and has to defend himself, then he is likely to become indignant and resentful, and your evaluation procedure will have done more harm than good. Help him to develop a plan to improve his performance where necessary.

How you conduct your meeting will determine if the employee leaves it with resentment, or whether he understands that you are genuinely concerned about his problems, as well as his performance. There are three major points to cover during the interview:

1. How is he doing

This is where you compare his actual performance against the standards you have set for the job and the expectations you have for him. Many managers find objective measurement is difficult, because likes and dislikes, as well as personal prejudices, enter into their appraisals. But it does require an objective and fair review of what he has accomplished well, where he has failed, where he is below expectations, and what steps he can take to improve.

2. What is expected

So many failures in job performance can be traced directly to the fact that the employee has never been properly instructed in what was expected of him. Perhaps the original job instructions were misunderstood, or perhaps another supervisor came along who had different ideas and methods from his predecessor, *but no one told the staff of the new standards.* Sounds impossible but it *does* happen.

If staff are to be expected to perform at peak they must know exactly what management expects from them. If there are doubts about an employee understanding his duties have him write out his interpretation of them, what he thinks is expected of him, and what he believes would be a good standard of performance. You can then go over this job description with him and correct any points of disagreement.

3. How can he improve

This is where you offer guidance by going over those areas requiring improvement and explaining why and how they should be improved. Let your employee know that you are concerned for his career as well as his effectiveness to your agency.

Handling Employee Reaction to Your Evaluation

Most successful employees will accept your evaluation, even though they might express surprise at some aspects of it. Where the employee does agree with you, you must satisfy yourself that such agreement is genuine, because many people tend to hide behind an easy agreement when criticized. Sometimes an employee refuses to agree with you. If he is stubborn about it at the first meeting, let it ride for a day or two, and schedule another meeting several days later. Try to discover the reasons for disagreement, then review them carefully, and if they are valid, be prepared to change your evaluation.

Without forcing the issue, try to get the employee to accept your evaluation of him. If you have his respect, then this is relatively simple to accomplish, because he knows you are guiding him for his own good. You will find that if he accepts your evaluation, the relationship between you and he will be closer, and you will also find it is easier to work with each other in the future.

Remember that when you talk with subordinates about their performance, it must be constructive and not demeaning. Your employees are the most important assets of your agency, so it is to your advantage to do all that you can to improve their skills by realistic appraisals and helpful suggestions and guidance.

14. HOW TO GIVE AN ORDER

It is physically impossible for the busy travel agency manager to do everything himself, so he must accomplish work assignments and goals by working through others. The basic function of a manager is to instruct and direct the work of subordinates—in other words, the good manager gets things done through people. The manner in which you give instructions to your staff (and the ingredient for success in giving those instructions) lies in the difference between being a leader and a driver.

If you still practice the old-fashioned autocratic method of management, you will soon discover that few employees react well to a driver. If you are an autocrat, you will more than likely have low morale in your office, as well as a high turnover of staff. To give an order is one thing—*all* managers must issue instructions and directions to those whom they supervise. But if the employees look upon your instructions as commands that allow little or no consideration of their feelings, they will become resentful, frustrated, and possibly resistant.

On the other hand, the manager who leads employees can expect tremendous results by giving his instructions in an easy and informal manner. They appear more like requests than commands, even though they are still orders.

There are certain techniques for giving orders, and the good manager knows that *how* he gives them will determine how well they are carried out. He knows that the majority of people today welcome leadership, and so they only need to be asked in a polite manner for them to accomplish the job properly.

There are basically four types of orders:

1. The suggestion
2. The request
3. The command
4. The call for volunteers

MANAGING YOUR STAFF

The Suggestion

When you use this technique, it carries just as much weight as a direct command, but under most circumstances it will not antagonize as much as the command will. By using the suggestion, you are not driving the employee, but you are exploiting his desire to be a follower, a trait that is inherent in most of those who are not leaders.

When you make a suggestion, take the time to explain the reasons for it, because if the employee knows *why* he is doing a job, he will then be able to determine if he is doing it correctly. It might be necessary for you to explain *how* a job is to be done, but leave this to the employee if you can. If he is given the opportunity to exercise his initiative, the chances are that the job will be accomplished much quicker and more efficiently than if he is given directions down to the last detail.

The Request

This type of order will probably be the most frequent one you will issue. It, too, carries the weight of the command, but gives the employee some freedom of action, and he can question any part that he misunderstands or about which he requires further information. It also allows him to include his own ideas. The request is not quite so loose as a suggestion nor as rigid as a command.

The Command

There will be cases where it is necessary to give a direct command. *How* you give it will determine how well it will be carried out. If you make an employee so nervous that he is afraid of making a mistake, you will certainly not accomplish the desired result. Try to avoid the "do this" and "do that" approach if at all possible, as it is likely to build up resentment.

The Call for Volunteers

This type of order is sometimes used in getting tasks accomplished that employees are reluctant to undertake—but the job must still get done. An example might be, "I need help on this filing job, would anybody like to help out."

The Six Components of an Order

1. *Who* is to do the job
2. *What* is to be done
3. *When* is it to start
4. *Where* is the work to be done
5. *How* is the work to be done
6. *Why* is the work to be done

The Five Rules for Giving Orders

1. Give the reason

To keep your staff interested and to help them understand, let them know what is going on, and give them the reason you want a certain task performed in a specific manner. We all want to know why things are done one way as opposed to another, and we all want to know for what we are building and the end result.

2. Confidence

Let your employees know that *you* know what they are doing, and let them have no doubts as to your ability and knowledge. You can convey confidence in your eyes, by your posture and general manner, by the tone of your voice when you give instructions, and by a friendly attitude. These are all mannerisms that help you get the idea across.

3. Firmness and Tact

No matter how unpleasant an order might be, never apologize for having to give it, and combine firmness with tact. Never let an employee talk you out of an order or allow him to change your mind, because if you do, your effectiveness will be greatly diminished. Be firm, polite and considerate, and accept total responsibility for your orders.

4. Clear, Concise Instructions

When giving any order or instruction, be certain that the person understands *exactly* what it is you want done. Most problems that surround the incorrect performance of an assigned task are the *fault of the manager* and not of the employee. You cannot, in all fairness, expect a person to do a job unless you explain it to him properly. If there is doubt that the employee has failed to grasp the instructions, ask him to repeat them back to you.

5. Follow-up

To satisfy yourself that the job was completed, it is always a good idea to follow up on your orders. If your orders were not carried out properly, you will have to find out why, so you can correct the situation. If the job was well-done, be sure to compliment the employee, and let him know of your approval.

General Guidelines and Review

1. Give orders clearly, and not only so that they are understood *but so they cannot possibly be misunderstood.*
2. Know the job you are assigning.
3. Avoid confusion—only give one or two orders at a time.

4. Assign the work to the proper employee.
5. Allow adequate time for the work to be performed.
6. If the assignment is complex, demonstrate.
7. Do not confuse—give adequate details.
8. Give your orders through the proper channels. For example, if there is another supervisor between you and the employee, go through the supervisor. If you by-pass another supervisor, you are liable to set up a morale problem with *him*.
9. Keep your instructions on a professional level. Always avoid sarcasm and other forms of antagonism.
10. Always follow through.

15. HOW TO TAKE DISCIPLINARY ACTION

Sooner or later every manager comes upon a situation requiring disciplinary action due to some sin of commission or omission on the part of an employee. No one really enjoys taking an employee to task, but when an employee fails in some area of his responsibilities, then the manager—if he is to remain in control—must take corrective action. "Action" could consist of a mild reprimand, or in its extreme form, might mean instant dismissal of the person involved.

The Warning

When you discover a situation that requires corrective action, the first step is to warn the employee that he has erred. It is only fair to first tell someone that they are doing something wrong, as all employees have the right to know when they are not measuring up so that they can take steps to improve their performance. A friendly warning will, in most cases, be the end of the matter. Who knows—it might even improve the relationship between you and the employee. By telling the employee where he stands, you will at least have gained his respect, if not his approval. Everyone knows that unless there are rules in operating a business there would be chaos. People also respect a manager who administers his office and his staff fairly, impartially, and consistently.

You will have to use your best judgment to determine the degree of warning required. If you know and understand each of your employees you will know if a friendly word in an informal way will do the trick, or whether you must resort to stronger measures. If an employee realizes that he has been careless he will probably correct his own shortcomings anyway.

With a warning, there is no threat made on an employee's job, as everything is generally kept on a firm but informal basis. If the situation fails to improve, then you will have to go a step further and issue an ultimatum. Here is where you tell the employee that unless specific improvements are made by a specific date, you will have to take additional action such as a pay cut, a demotion, perhaps even termination. Such an ultimatum places the responsibility on the employee to reform.

Know the Person

Fit your approach to the individual. Is he sensitive? Will you create resentment? Does he require encouragement in his job? Temper your remarks and the manner in which you handle the situation to the employee. If you know your employees well (and you should), you will be able to judge the right degree of disciplinary action for each one.

Get the Facts

Before you call an employee on the carpet, *get all of the facts.* It is essential that you be accurate in your assessment of the problem when you confront an employee, so that he will realize that you are serious and have taken the time and trouble to discover the precise nature of the problem. Deal only in specifics and never in generalities.

Know the Cause

Why is performance below the norm? Is it *really* the employee's fault, or does the problem have something to do with the company and its policies? Does the employee normally turn in a reasonably good performance, or is he habitually a poor worker? Perhaps he has unknown problems which affect his job performance.

Be Objective

Too many managers tend to take a dislike to an employee and allow this dislike to influence their judgment. Be certain to treat all of your employees alike when you discipline. Never single out one for harsher treatment than another for the same offense. If you are under pressure or in an irritable mood, delay disciplining until you can be more objective.

Timing

If you are angry when you discipline you will have lost your judgment, as well as your impartiality. Wait until you cool down.

Listen

Give your employee ample opportunity to tell his side of the story without interruption. Be sure to get the *whole* story before you make your decision on how to handle the situation.

Solution

If the employee's performance is below the expectations and standards you have established, tell him what he must do in order to improve. If all that you do is to tell him that he *must* improve, he might not be too sure how to go about it. Try to help him by giving him a step-by-step self-improvement program.

Follow up

Always follow up. If the employee has improved, then encourage him by telling him so, and let him know you have observed his progress and are taking an interest in it. Conversely, if he ignores your warning, then you will probably have to take further action, because if you overlook it or let it slide, the problem will not be solved—only magnified.

Poor Performance

If you set specific standards of performance and an employee is not meeting them, you must discover the reason. If the job has not been properly explained to him, if he does not know what to do, or if he does not know what he is doing, then it is not his fault. The fault is with the manager, rather than with the employee who cannot possibly meet standards until the supervisor sets them.

It is important to take adequate time to properly and thoroughly instruct the employee in his work and to tell him exactly what standards you expect. If the employee lacks the ability to perform the job on your terms and standards, then an early parting of the ways is probably best for all concerned. If the employee is lazy, then you will have to go into the warning routine—no manager likes to have a loafer around.

Petty Infractions

These are usually more of an irritant than they are a serious issue, but over a period of time (if they are allowed to continue) they can build up into major problems. *Warnings are essential when the infractions occur*—never let them pass without action because if you do, they will become much harder to solve.

Poor Attitude

Just because an employee is competent in the performance of the job does not necessarily mean that he is an ideal employee for your office. If he is surly, short tempered, uncooperative, resentful of taking orders, and difficult for you and the rest of the staff to get along with, there is little choice but to take corrective action.

Schedule a private meeting with the employee, and outline the specific problems requiring improvement and correction. Give him a reasonable but brief period to make the adjustment, but at the same time, let him know that if he fails to improve to your complete satisfaction that he will be terminated, demoted, or suffer whatever other penalty you consider to be necessary.

Serious Offenses

If an employee has committed a serious infraction he should be terminated on the spot. Giving someone "another chance" might be satisfactory for a minor violation, but to do so for stealing, dishonesty, criminal acts, etc. can only expose your agency to considerable hazards which in turn might cause financial losses, or worse.

Discipline Guidelines

1. Investigate conditions *before* you criticize, then base your handling of the situation only on known facts and not on suppositions and assumptions.
2. Correct without anger. Always be patient, calm and tactful.
3. Never single out any one individual and make an "example." If there has been a slackening of discipline throughout the office, then place the responsibility for improvement upon everyone. This is best handled at a meeting of all involved.
4. Be certain that you or the company are not responsible for the need to correct an employee. If you have been, be willing to admit it.
5. Avoid being personal. Let the employee know that it is the actual *infraction* that is being condemned and not him as a *person*.
6. Never belittle or anger an employee or make him feel inferior. If you do, you will only create resentment.

Some Serious Offenses

tardiness	garnishments
absenteeism	inefficiency
inaccuracy	poor attitude
carelessness	low output
insubordination	rudeness

Handle these, and other serious violations not listed here, by determining whether the employee has been properly instructed and an attempt made to improve. Go to the "early warning system," and tell the employee what will happen to him if he fails to improve, or if he continues to break the same rules over and over again. If there is no improvement by the time limit you set, you will then have to take corrective action through punishment.

Some Severe Offenses

gambling	lying
stealing	intoxication on the job
dishonesty	rudeness to clients
criminal acts	falsifying company records
continued insubordination	willful damage to company property, etc.

Most of these require immediate discharge *without warning,* as the chances are that if he has committed any of these acts once, then he might do so again. You cannot afford to take chances.

16. HOW TO HANDLE EMPLOYEE COMPLAINTS

In the day-to-day operation of any business, mistakes will occur, and no manager can possibly please all of the staff all of the time. Sooner or later, even the most efficient and well-run office will encounter problems, and complaints will arise from employees.

You really only have two choices in the handling of complaints:

1. Forget about them. (Perhaps they will go away!)
2. Handle them promptly and in a manner fair to all concerned.

Is there really more than one logical choice? No, because if a complaint goes unheeded, what started off as something relatively insignificant will tend to feed on itself, and before you know what happened it will have grown out of all proportion to the complaint. If you ignore it it will spawn other problems, and you will then have not one issue to settle but a dozen—many of which will be unrelated to the original grievance.

Delay in handling or solving a complaint can cause loss of output, unrest among the staff, perhaps resignations, and even a loss of face on your part and loss of respect toward you.

Get into the habit of handling all complaints quickly and efficiently as soon as they appear. Perhaps you cannot break away from what you happen to be doing at the precise moment the employee walks in with a problem, but let your staff know that you are anxious to solve problems as soon as you can. Immediate settlement is not always possible, anyway, as some complaints are far too complex for instant solutions. One, perhaps two days at the most should be adequate time to dispose of most of the complaints emanating from your staff.

Encourage complaints, because if you suppress them, the employees will still harbor them, and there will be an undercurrent of unrest in the office, which in turn will lead to a breakdown of morale. Besides, if you get complaints, you will then have a good idea as to what is going on in the minds of your staff. If there are no complaints, your staff are either unusually content or it might indicate that your staff lacks confidence in you, or are even afraid of you (an intolerable situation).

Complaints are usually caused by an employee's dissatisfaction, either real or fancied, so be on the alert for some of the symptoms and indicators of unrest. There are any number of reliable signs that indicate all is not well in the office. Remember, too, that complaints are *caused,* they do not just happen.

Some Symptoms of Dissatisfaction

Here is a list of some of the more common symptoms of unrest. Watch for them, and should they appear, be prepared to recognize them for what they are, then move fast to solve the problem.

long lunch breaks	avoidance of assignment
tardiness	loafing
sullenness	dislike of the job

belligerency and insubordination
frequent illness
nervous tension
lack of interest

petty gripes to colleagues
unusual number of errors
frustration and fear
insecurity

Some Causes of Complaints

unsatisfactory working conditions
desk too small
lack of filing space
inadequate restroom facilities
uneven distribution of work
not enough overtime
work assignments beyond capabilities
unfairness
too much pressure
demanding more than employee can produce
aloofness
failure to gain promotion
suspension
illness
marital and domestic trouble
boy friend or girl friend problems
unsatisfactory diet
temperamentally unsuited for the job

inadequate training for the job
too hot or too cold
outmoded typewriter
poor lighting
too much overtime
work too easy
poor supervision
supervisor playing favorites
promises not kept
lack of guidance
stealing credit
a demotion
financial problems
consistently poor health
other family problems
drugs
lack of sleep
emotionally immature
excessive eating and drinking habits

As you can see, there is no shortage of reasons from which to choose when it comes time for an employee to complain, and those listed here are only *some* of the more common ones. Try to get to know each employee as well as you can. Know his background as well as his capabilities and his failings. Be alert to obvious changes in attitude toward you, other members of the staff, and the clients. If you are aware of what is going on around you as it relates to your subordinates, then you are performing one of the most important functions of a good manager. The more you know about each member of your staff and of his or her capabilities, the quicker you can settle disputes, solve problems and complaints, and maintain harmony in your office. No office can function efficiently unless it operates smoothly, and if problems do develop they should be settled promptly before they get out of hand and become enlarged out of all proportion.

When a member of your staff comes to you to complain:

1. Receive the complaint.
2. Get the facts.
3. Take corrective action.
4. Follow up.

How you handle the situation and receive a complaint will have an effect upon its solution. Listen carefully to what the employee has to say, and above all remain calm and take notes if necessary. Get the story accurately, and get to the heart of the matter. You must have all of the data at your fingertips if you are ever to solve the problem effectively.

After the employee has had his say, go over the major points with him to be certain that you have everything straight and that you thoroughly understand exactly what the problem is. If you cannot solve the problem immediately, tell your employee when he can expect an answer, and do it as soon as you can because until you settle the matter, your employee will still harbor the problem within himself.

If the complaint is a valid one, do everything you can to settle it to the employee's satisfaction, but if you cannot do so, let him know why. If the employee has no basis for his complaint, you will probably have to convince him of this, and this might take time. If you or the company is in the wrong, then be prepared to admit it.

Be certain to follow up later to ensure that your decision has been followed and that another complaint cannot emanate from the same source. If you find that the employee *still* feels he was right and you were wrong in your decision over his complaint, then you have not settled it. Try to resolve it as soon as you can.

The Chronic Complainer

If you are unlucky enough to have a chronic complainer on your staff, then you have a problem which is not so simple to solve. The major difficulty is that the chronic complainer is not always sure of what it is he is complaining about. He is a generally unhappy individual and always has *something* to gripe about—most of the time without a valid reason. More important, and more dangerous, he attempts to influence others in the office.

This type of complainer requires immediate and drastic action, because unless you solve it quickly, you are likely to end up with more than one problem and more than one complainer. First, try to convince him that he must stop his petty griping, and give him a time limit in which to stop—a day or two at the most. Unless you can reform him fast you are much better off terminating him without further delay. The damage a chronic complainer can do in an office often is beyond repair, and you cannot afford him, no matter how good he may be at his job.

17. DEALING WITH THE PROBLEM EMPLOYEE

Many managers will never admit to having staff problems, because such a situation often reflects upon the ability of the manager. In almost every office events can occur which cause an employee to become a problem, resulting in turmoil not only for the manager but for the entire office.

Often the employee becomes a problem because of contributing factors outside of himself, so when you investigate a problem member of your staff, remember to analyze the total situation and discover *why* he is acting the way he is. Get to the bottom of it, for only when you have all of the facts can you attempt corrective action.

If the problems are personal ones, such as financial difficulties, marital or emotional problems, or mental disorders, they are known as "person-centered," and there is not much you can do about them except to offer help, sympathy and guidance. But if the problems are caused by the company or the manager, they are office-oriented, and there is much the alert manager can do to eliminate them.

First Define the Problem

Once you have located the *source,* you can take fast action to arriving at a fair conclusion. There are a variety of factors which have a bearing on whether a person is likely to become a problem, and it will help you to know what they are.

Lack of Skills

It is not unusual for a good employee to become a problem because he lacks the skills and experience to competently perform the tasks assigned to him, and is unable to meet the standard of performance expected of him. If an employee is assigned a job that he cannot complete or perform because he is deficient in training, he will become frustrated, resentful and difficult to get along with. He might even antagonize clients, as well as suppliers such as carriers and tour operators. The moral here is never to place an employee in a position or situation where his training is insufficient to enable him to perform the job properly.

Poor Job Structure

If you ask an employee to perform a task that he had never been informed was his responsibility, or one where the duties have not been explained to him, then he can quite rightfully become resentful. He will probably blame the employer for his lack of knowledge, and both his morale and job performance will deteriorate. When you hire a new employee, explain the complete job in detail, then he will never be surprised when asked to do something unexpected.

Miscasting

If an employee is hired as an international counselor but then is assigned to a commercial account, he is obviously in the wrong job. This example might appear to be extreme, but it does illustrate the point. Be sure to place each employee in the job for which he is most skilled and enjoys most.

Inadequate Supervision

How well you actually supervise the office will determine whether you can expect staff problems. If supervision is too tight, your staff will be hampered in doing their jobs ("that manager never leaves me alone . . .

always standing over my shoulder"). If you are too lax, then some employees might be tempted to take advantage of what they think is an easy situation. Try to hit it just right—not too tight but not too loose, either.

An example of supervisory inconsistency would be where a specific policy was acceptable one day but not the next, or what was acceptable for one of the staff was not for another. Try to maintain the same level of supervision at all times, once you have set the policies and standards for your office.

Emotional Immaturity

There is very little you can do about this type of employee, because the problem is inherent with the person and is usually outside the jurisdiction or the capabilities of the manager to solve. If your office is large enough, try to keep the employee away from others as much as you can—something impossible to do in a small agency. If someone who is emotionally immature has to work closely with others, there is likely to be friction and dissent. You might have to terminate this type of person, or at least shock him by warning him that he will have to find another job unless he mends his ways.

Poor Health

It is usually possible to correct the lack of skills and many similar problems through training and counseling, but if an employee suffers from poor health, there is little or nothing a manager can do about it. The employee will worry about his ability to perform or continue with his job and will fret about his ability to continue to earn an income. Constant fear and worry will turn him into a problem, but it might be something with which you can live. If he is a valuable employee, and an asset to your agency, then by all means try to operate around his problem. Take the time to reassure him that his job is safe, and help him to overcome his fears.

Incompatibility

Perhaps "personality differences" would be a more appropriate term. Most of us are familiar with cases where two people just cannot seem to get along. The chemistry is not right, and they always seem to rub each other the wrong way. If you have an instance of incompatibility, each person must make a serious attempt to get along for the good of the agency, for the good of their careers, and for the good of the entire office. If they cannot learn to live with each other in the office, then you will probably have to let one of them go.

Avoiding People Problems

The best time to discover who is likely to become a problem is during the hiring process, and if you follow all of the steps in the total hiring process, you will be able to eliminate those who are potential problem employees.

Good supervision comes under the heading of human relations, and it is essential that all of your employees blend together. Each is just one cog in the machine. People also want to be recognized by their supervisor, as well as their peers. No one wants to be part of a group forever, and most of us want to get ahead in our careers.

Here are the keys to avoiding people problems:

1. Maintain proper discipline.
2. Evaluate performance.
3. Let the employee know where he stands at all times.
4. Use your evaluation procedure to detect problem employees early.
5. Revamp the employee's job if necessary and practical.
6. Help employees with their problems whenever possible.
7. Recognize your employees as individuals.
8. Understand each employee.

PART 3
Managing Yourself

18. WHAT MAKES A GOOD SUPERVISOR

The travel marketplace is a highly competitive one, and as the travel industry continues to grow, and retail travel agencies proliferate, it is expected that the industry will become even more competitive in the future.

While it is essential to possess all of the academic knowledge and expertise of travel, travel knowledge in itself is no longer sufficient to manage a travel agency in today's highly competitive and complex business climate. All too many travel agencies stagnate, or fail completely simply because the management was mediocre, or the manager lacked the required management and business skills necessary to lead an agency down the paths of growth and profitability.

While there are many criteria that go into the overall make-up of a good manager, most of them will be found in one or another of the six basic ingredients for successful management:

1. Positive mental attitude
2. Creative ability
3. Administrative skills
4. Courage
5. Judgment
6. Character

As we examine these characteristics in more depth, compare how you yourself rate with each one, so that you can acquire those traits you now lack.

Positive Mental Attitude

A supervisor—any supervisor—must radiate genuine and sincere enthusiasm and confidence. Any successful operation must be led by a supervisor who has faith and pride in his work, his goals, and in his ability to accomplish those goals.

It is not always an easy task to maintain a positive disposition all of the time, especially in the face of adversity or defeat. But optimism must always show through the difficulties and failures that often occur in business.

Keep in mind at all times that a positive mental attitude can carry you and your company on to new achievements, while a lack of it will create a negative environment which will tend to attract disaster and failure. Avoid pessimism at all costs, and keep away from those negative thinkers who say a new idea will never work "because it has never been done that way before." Our world is teeming with successful products and services created by visionaries who were assured by "experts" that their ideas were unpractical and would not work.

When your optimism flags, go to your nearest bookstore and acquire books on the subjects of success and motivation. Outstanding authors include Dr. Norman Vincent Peale, W. Clement Stone and Napolean Hill. There are many other works, and a good bookstore will offer an excellent selection. To be successful in whatever you do, first purge yourself of negative thoughts, then stand back and watch results.

Creative Ability

Business today requires men and women who can think, because absolutely nothing starts without an idea. A good supervisor must have the ability to think clearly as well as creatively. The fast-moving pattern of modern business demands it, if success and profitability are to be attained.

Administrative Skill

This is the dull side of the supervisor's job. It requires constant attention to a host of details, as well as supervisory and decision-making responsibilities in day-to-day operations. It is also necessary to look into the future and try to forecast requirements in terms of money, time, manpower and materials.

Courage

Every time we take a step in a new direction or try something different we are being courageous. Successful managers must be willing to gamble and to incur *some* risks in business, as we can never own complete information upon which to base sound decisions. Moving into a new venture or a new tour program requires a course of positive action, because if we wait some other enterprising competitor might seize the opportunity and do it first. When it is time to advance, a supervisor must have the courage of his convictions, though this does not mean that he should move without careful thought and planning.

It takes courage to delegate responsibility, because in the final analysis, *accountability for results cannot be delegated.* When we delegate to subordinates, we must do so knowing that it is the supervisor who must accept the blame if plans go awry.

Judgment

True leaders must make sound and wise decisions based upon the knowledge and facts of given situations available to them. Supervisors must make judgments every day. Some judgments will be based on known facts, while others will be made based upon incomplete data and information. Good old common sense (another term for judgment) must be called upon to weigh each factor before a decision is reached.

We all make errors in judgment sometimes—no one has a perfect score. Remember, too, that negative thinking is not a substitute for judgment, and that enthusiasm is a vital requirement of a leader who must make frequent judgments and decisions.

Character

The qualities of honesty, sincerity and integrity must be unquestionable—there can be no compromise. The good supervisor must possess these traits if he is to earn the respect and support of his employees, clients and suppliers. Today's intense competition spawns all manner of unethical practices, but how ever many times you have experienced deceit, fraud, dishonesty, misrepresentation and other chicanery, never let these experiences affect your own integrity.

There Is No Perfection

These six qualities are hardly ever achieved to their fullest extent in any one person. Anyone who wishes to excel in management must first analyze himself, then evaluate his characteristics, strengths and weaknesses. Only then can he build and develop in the areas in which he is interested.

The Good Supervisor Traits

The good supervisor will already possess many of these characteristics, all of which are essential in management positions. Check off those that apply to you, then try to attain the remainder as soon as you can.

The good supervisor:

— Treats his staff like people, and makes them feel they are working with him, rather than for him.
— Has earned the respect of his staff.

- Keeps his staff advised on their progress, and helps them solve their problems and overcome their failings.
- Never talks down to his staff; treats them as equals.
- Treats all employees alike, and does not have favorites.
- Encourages his employees to submit their ideas and suggestions, and uses them whenever he can.
- Helps his employees understand their jobs and their responsibilities, and assists them to develop their potential.
- Pays careful attention to morale, recognizing that high morale is essential for the success of his business.
- Is accurate and clear in giving work assignments, and makes certain that employees understand what is expected of them.
- Is always fair and honest with his employees, and expects the same treatment in return.
- Always listens to his employees when they come to him with a problem or complaint, and respects and recognizes their side of it.
- Always handles complaints quickly.
- Displays tolerance, patience, dependability, cheerfulness and optimism.
- Keeps his employees advised and informed on changes of policy, new systems, and new methods of operation.
- Is a man of his word; his employees know they can trust him to keep his promises.
- Knows his own capabilities and shortcomings.
- Knows how to delegate responsibility.
- Enjoys his job.
- Is a good planner and organizer, and can also plan the work for his office and assist his staff in planning their work, too.
- Accepts challenges with a positive attitude, and enjoys overcoming problems.
- Is flexible, possesses drive, ambition, and is always seeking new and better ways of doing things.
- Keeps up-to-date on all new techniques, fare structure changes, new products, and ensures that his employees know about them.

19. THE MANAGER'S RESPONSIBILITIES

A manager, or supervisor, is one who gets things done through people. In other words, he is responsible for the work of others. The supervisor is the medium by which orders, instructions and information flow downward; and suggestions, information and problems flow upward. He must lead his people rather than drive them, and he must direct their work, help them to develop their skills, and assist them in improving their job performance. While he may delegate specific tasks to others, *he cannot delegate accountability for the results of those below him.*

This section is a job description of the typical supervisor. It represents basic responsibilities and functions engaged in by managers, no matter how large or small a company may be, or how many employees are supervised.

Responsibilities of a Supervisor

Plans, directs and coordinates the work of those under him.
Motivates, trains and develops subordinates to improve their performance, and prepares them to assume greater responsibility.
Controls the quantity and quality of work.
Maintains discipline and morale of his staff.
Maintains satisfactory working conditions.
Communicates information to subordinates and superiors.
Recommends promotions, demotions, discharges and other changes in job classification.
Evaluates work flow; makes changes for improvement.
Evaluates job performance of subordinates.
Approves or rejects job applicants after screening.
Reports to next level of management.

Responsibilities Checklist

The following list of more detailed responsibilities can be used to determine if you are performing the *complete* job as manager.

Self-development

Prepare for greater responsibilities.
Accept and take more responsibility when opportunity occurs.
Know the job of each subordinate.
Know the company's policies, rules and goals.
Maintain self-control at all times.
Set a good example through good leadership.
Read management books and/or take study courses to improve all functions of management skills.

In Relation to Subordinates

Assign work to best qualified.
Ensure that each employee knows what to do and why.
Train new employees.
Encourage initiative, and help others assume responsibility.
Evaluate the performance of others.

Know each person's capabilities.
Encourage suggestions for the improvement of the office.
Give credit in public to those to whom it is due.
Train employees for greater responsibility.
Develop harmony and teamwork.
Develop skills of subordinates.
Take a personal interest in all whom you supervise.
Build and maintain morale.
Earn the respect and confidence of subordinates.
Provide equitable treatment of all employees.
Maintain discipline.
Correct false rumors and circulation of unverified stories.
Learn how to handle each individual according to personality differences inherent in each of us.
Interview and screen all new employees.
Control absenteeism.
Control personal frictions and jealousies among employees.
Reprimand tactfully.
Keep all staff advised of changes in the office, new procedures, revised rules, etc.
Give all orders in a clear and concise manner.

In Relation to Superiors

Assist superior in every way possible.
Understand exactly what superior wants done.
Keep superior informed of all results and progress.
Accept full responsibility for the work of the staff.
Avoid shifting blame to others.
Organize to avoid wasting time.
Ensure superior's orders are carried out properly.
Report on quality and quantity of work.
On those matters requiring superior's attention, be certain they are referred to him promptly.
Pass on ideas for improvement, and give credit to those to whom it is due.
Keep cost of doing business within budget.
Ensure all work is completed on time.
Ensure that quality and quantity of work are maintained.
Ensure that all work is performed accurately.
Set standards for all positions supervised.
Anticipate problems.
Meet and minimize peak work loads.
Be alert for new ideas and systems.
Keep pace with changing conditions.

As you can see, the job of supervisor is a broad one; perfection in all these responsibilities is rare, but none should be overlooked.

20. MANAGEMENT PERFORMANCE SELF-EVALUATION

This self-evaluation has been designed to help you help yourself. By itself, it has no worth, but it can be of tremendous value to those who are seriously interested in developing and improving their management skills and abilities.

If you are already using your talents to the maximum, or if you believe that you are experienced beyond improvement, *stop right here*. But if you think that you have abilities that are not being used in the course of your responsibilities, this self-evaluation can be of tremendous value. But you must possess the *desire* to do a better job, and you must have the *objectivity* to be able to evaluate yourself honestly.

The longest journey in the world commences with a single step, and the starting point for any improvement program is acknowledgement of the *need* to improve. If we really want to be candid with ourselves, we can all improve ourselves in some measure. If you own and operate your own agency, you will want assurance that you are on the right track to good management; in fact if you fail to recognize the symptoms of bad management you may go out of business. If you are employed by a larger organization your progress will depend upon your performance of your *present* responsibilities. Because of intense competition in the business world of today, no one in a management or supervisory position can allow himself the luxury of mediocre performance, or of performing at a level that is less than his very best.

Answering the Questions

1. Be certain you have read the question and understand what it asks.
2. Circle the letter at the right of the page that compares with the answer that comes closest to the truth. You are not restricted to one answer per question—if you wish to indicate several choices, do so.
3. Be completely honest with yourself, because if you are not, you won't get an accurate evaluation of your performance, and the test will be for naught. Remember, the ability of a man to analyze his work and evaluate his job performance realistically is indicative of his maturity of judgment and his readiness for increased responsibilities.
4. Avoid the temptation to look at the evaluation on page 74 until you have completed all of the questions.

1. How would you classify your ability to manage?
   a. Better than most
   b. A little better than most
   c. Average
   d. Below average
   e. Unsatisfactory
   f. Don't know

2. How would you rate yourself as to *volume* of work?
   a. Very high
   b. Better than most
   c. Average
   d. Low volume
   e. Doing nothing
   f. Don't know

3. How would you rate yourself on *quality* of work?
   a. Very high
   b. Better than most
   c. Average
   d. Low quality
   e. Poor quality
   f. Don't know

4. How well do you express yourself?
   a. Very well
   b. Better than most
   c. About average
   d. Worse than most
   e. Poorly
   f. Don't know

5. Do you consider yourself a good manager?
   a. Very definitely
   b. I think I am
   c. Almost
   d. I doubt that I am
   e. Am not going to try
   f. Don't know

6. How much self-discipline do you have?
   a. Much more than most
   b. More than most
   c. About average
   d. Less than average
   e. None
   f. Don't know

7. How effectively do you use your working time?
   a. Never waste a minute
   b. Better than most
   c. About average
   d. Below average
   e. Poorly
   f. Don't know

MANAGING YOURSELF 71

8. How easy is it for your subordinates to talk to you?
   a. Very easy
   b. Fairly easy
   c. We get along
   d. When they must
   e. Very hard
   f. Don't know

9. If a subordinate comes to you with a complaint, how do you handle it?
   a. Immediately
   b. As soon as I can
   c. Fairly quickly
   d. Delay it
   e. Never
   f. Don't know

10. How well do you accept subordinates' suggestions?
    a. The more, the better
    b. I welcome them
    c. I try to make use of them
    d. I resent them
    e. They make me angry
    f. Don't know

11. How does the quality of your ideas compare with others?
    a. Better than others
    b. Generally good ideas
    c. As good as the rest
    d. Poorer than average
    e. Very poor ideas
    f. Don't know

12. What kind of self-improvement program do you pursue?
    a. Study every day
    b. Have planned program
    c. Read when I can
    d. Read occasional articles
    e. Don't need one
    f. Don't know

13. What plans do you have for acquiring more knowledge?
    a. Degree or diploma
    b. Night or trade school
    c. Planned program
    d. Informal reading
    e. No plans
    f. Don't need any more

14. To what extent do you read books on good management techniques?
    a. Most of them
    b. A good many
    c. One a month
    d. Once in a while
    e. When I have time
    f. Never have time

15. How well did you meet last
    year's goals and plans?
    a. Very well
    b. Better than expected
    c. About what I expected
    d. Worse than expected
    e. Dismal failure
    f. Don't know

16. How frequently do you examine
    your goals and revise plans
    to meet changing situations?
    a. Monthly
    b. Quarterly
    c. Semi-annually
    d. Sometimes
    e. Haphazardly
    f. Never

17. If a major problem develops,
    how do you handle it?
    a. Immediately
    b. Next day
    c. As soon as I can
    d. I put it off
    e. Delegate it
    f. Never, hope it goes away

18. How well do you delegate
    responsibility?
    a. Frequently
    b. Whenever I can
    c. Once in a while
    d. When asked
    e. Hardly ever
    f. Never, don't trust anyone

19. Good or bad, how many ideas
    do you get that are appli-
    cable to your work?
    a. A great number of ideas
    b. Many ideas
    c. As many ideas as most
    d. Less than average number
    e. No ideas
    f. Don't know

20. When you are the only one
    who can and should make an
    important decision, how do
    you handle it?
    a. Decide immediately
    b. Decide fairly quickly
    c. Decide as soon as I can
    d. Appoint a study committee
    e. Delegate it
    f. Forget about it

21. In management or staff
    meetings, do you speak
    up with your ideas and
    opinions?
    a. Always
    b. Frequently
    c. Sometimes
    d. Hardly ever
    e. Afraid to
    f. Never

22. How well do you accept your superior's suggestions for improvement of your work?
   a. The more the better
   b. They are good for me
   c. I try to use them
   d. I resent them
   e. They make my angry
   f. Don't know

23. How well would you rate your relationship with your superior?
   a. Could not be better
   b. Very good
   c. As good as any
   d. We get along
   e. Poor
   f. Downright bad

PLEASE DON'T TURN THIS PAGE UNTIL YOU HAVE ANSWERED ALL OF THE QUESTIONS.

INSTRUCTIONS

Total the number of a's you have circled and place this total in the appropriate place below. Do the same with b, c, and so on until all of your answers are collated.

Total a._____
Total b._____
Total c._____
Total d._____
Total e._____
Total f._____

The letter with the largest number against it indicates your *present level of performance*. The letter with the second highest number indicates the *direction your performance is likely to go in the future*. With this newly acquired knowledge you now have the ability to determine your future in your career, and to take the steps necessary to improve those management functions requiring polishing.

You can now turn the page and review the evaluation section on the next page. A discussion of each performance level is given so you can understand where you are and in which direction you are heading.

EVALUATION

a. IDEAL—It is altogether unrealistic to expect anyone to perform at this level. There may be one or two points in this area, and if so, that is excellent. They indicate peaks of performance that are rare in most individuals.

b. BETTER THAN AVERAGE—If you fall into this category you are above the norm, and all you need do is to review your overall performance and polish up what you are already doing well. It should take only minimal effort to be recognized as exceptional. Just don't stop now.

c. AVERAGE—Most of us will end up in this group. This is the middle of the road, and by definition indicates mediocrity. Average performance is only acceptable and safe if all is going well with the company, or with the business trend in general. When problems arise, or the going gets rough, this area tends to lose some of its security. Let someone else be mediocre.

d. BELOW AVERAGE—In some cases this may be an acceptable performance, but comes dangerously close to not doing the job. This is only just getting by. If you have any d's circled better take a close look at them, and commence improvement as soon as you can.

e. LOW PERFORMANCE—If you find yourself in this group, there is a serious problem somewhere along the line. It is unlikely that a person could get to this point in his career and not have the ability to perform better. If you are in business for yourself, chances are you won't be much longer. If you work for someone else you *could* find yourself out of a job. In any event, get help—from your superior or someone who can guide you.

f. SPECIAL CASE—Generally speaking if you have items in this section you are probably out of touch with reality, or are in the wrong job. You probably either don't have the necessary expertise in management functions or have no communication with your superior. Get help fast.

Development isn't something that is done to an individual . . .
It is something that he does to himself.

APPENDIX
A Travel Agency Policy Manual

Note: This Policy Manual can be adapted by any agency and is an example of the type of policies which should be spelled out to avoid possible problems and misunderstandings. It was adapted from one in use by Wheaton Travel, Inc., Wheaton, Illinois.

I. DEFINITIONS
- A. Full-time Employee: One who works at least thirty-seven and one-half hours per week.
- B. Part-time Employee: One who works less than thirty-seven and one-half hours per week.
- C. Management: Chief executive officer and those designated by him for specific management responsibilities.
- D. Fiscal Year: February 1 through January 31.
- E. Employee Anniversary Date: The date on which employment begins.

II. OFFICE HOURS

The office will be open from 9:00 A.M. to 5:30 P.M. Monday through Friday and from 9:00 A.M. to 12:30 P.M. on Saturday. Exceptions to normal office hours will be Good Friday, Christmas Eve, and New Years Eve, which will follow the Saturday office schedule. Employees will be entitled to one hour for lunch on days they work at least seven and one-half hours.

Full-time employees are to report for work not later than 8:50 A.M.

Those employees who are scheduled for Saturday work are entitled to compensating time off. This time is to be taken on Tuesday, Wednesday, or Thursday in the week preceding that Saturday. No two counselors from the same department are to take their compensating time off during the same hours.

III. STAFF MEETINGS

Staff meetings will be held at 8:00 A.M., the first Monday of every even-numbered month, commencing with February, and otherwise as required by management. Such meetings are mandatory.

IV. PAID HOLIDAYS

Paid holidays are New Years Day, Memorial Day, Independence Day, Labor Day, Thanksgiving, and Christmas.

V. SICK LEAVE

An employee is entitled to five days' sick leave with pay within any fiscal year. Sick leave may be taken from the first day of employment. After these five sick days within the fiscal year, an amount equal to the hourly rate of compensation multiplied by the number of hours will be deducted from payroll check for time absent due to illness. For any unused sick leave within the fiscal year, an amount equal to four-tenths of one percent per unused sick day of the annual salary will be paid following the completion of a fiscal year.

Extended hospitalization or convalescence will be allowed up to a maximum of twenty-eight days without loss of seniority, points toward profit sharing, or other benefits.

VI. VACATION:

A. TIME ALLOWED: After a full-time employee has worked for one full year, he is entitled to two weeks paid vacation; after three full years of employment, three weeks vacation; and after five full years of employment, four weeks vacation.

B. VACATION NOT TAKEN: There will be no monetary compensation for vacation time not taken.

C. VACATION ACCRUAL: Vacation time cannot be borrowed from future years. Vacation time can be accrued provided an employee does not take more than four weeks in any given fiscal year.

D. VACATION PAY UPON TERMINATION: After the first year of employment, vacation time is earned in increments of six full months of employment. When employment is terminated, the employee shall receive compensation for unused vacation time based on the following:

Twelve Months	Two weeks earned
Twelve through Seventeen Months	Two weeks earned
Eighteen Months	Three weeks earned
Eighteen through Twenty-Three Months	Three weeks earned
Twenty-four Months	Four weeks earned

VII. OTHER EXCUSED LEAVE
   A. JURY DUTY: An employee will be reimbursed the difference between the gross amount received for jury duty and his normal salary for days of work missed.
   B. AIRLINE PRESENTATIONS; SEMINARS; FAMILIARIZATION TRIPS: Attendance at these activities and excused leave time for them will be at the discretion of management.
   C. MILITARY DUTY: An employee will be reimbursed the difference between the gross amount received for military obligations and his normal salary for days or work missed. Time allowed away from work for military obligation will be limited to two weeks within a fiscal year.
   D. MATERNITY LEAVE: An employee may take up to twenty-eight days maternity leave without pay.
   E. FUNERALS: Employees shall be allowed paid time off up to, but not to exceed, two work days (five in the case of a spouse) in addition to the day of notification of death in the immediate family. Immediate family consists of employees' parent, child, brother, sister, spouse, parents-in-law, grandparents, spouses grandparents, or any relative residing with the employee, or with whom the employee resides.

VIII. SALARY
   A. Payroll is every fourth Monday. There shall be thirteen pay periods within each fiscal year.
   B. SALARY ADVANCES: An employee may request a salary advance. Salary advances will be disbursed on the second Monday of a pay period.
   C. INCREASES: Increases will be February first and August first, based on commonly accepted cost-of-living increases. Management will also review performance at least once a year in consideration of possible salary increase attributed to merit.
   D. OVERTIME: Prior approval of management must be obtained prior to working overtime if the employee is to be compensated. Compensation for approved overtime will be monetary (based on the employee's hourly rate of pay as computed by the Accounting Department). Overtime is defined as any time over forty hours worked in a calendar week or over eight hours in a given day which has been previously approved for compensation.

IX. INSURANCE
   Current hospitalization insurance is offered through Massachusetts Mutual. This coverage is offered to an employee after thirty days of

employment are completed. To be eligible for this plan, an employee must work thirty hours per week. The Agency will pay one-half the amount of premium on single coverage or an amount equal to that toward a family policy. Premiums on life insurance coverage will be paid fully by the Agency. Coverage on life insurance is equal to one years salary. INSURANCE COVERAGE IS SUBJECT TO REVISION AT ANY TIME.

X. REDUCED RATE PRIVILEGES

A. ELIGIBILITY: Eligibility is determined by regulations set forth by A.T.C., I.A.T.A., Amtrak, and the International Passenger Ship Association.

B. DISTRIBUTION: Reduced rate privileges are distributed on the basis of need and availability, at the discretion of management.

XI. FAMILIARIZATION TRIPS

Eligibility, distribution, and excused leave from office for such trips will be at the discretion of management, based on the type of trip, requirements of tour operators, and work responsibility.

XII. PROFIT SHARING

"Profit-sharing" is better defined as that portion of the company's earnings which ownership chooses to share among its employees, based upon their tenure with the company. For the thirty-six months of full-time employment, one point is assigned. Thereafter, one point is assigned for each additional month of full-time employment. Credit is not given for any month or fraction thereof, for which a leave of absence has been granted. The total of all points assigned to all employees is then used to determine the employee's percentage of the whole. All payments of profit-sharing are subject to payroll tax deductions.

XIII. REIMBURSEMENT OF COMPANY EXPENSES

The company will reimburse an employee for expenses incurred in connection with job assignments or attendance at functions requested by management. Travel reimbursement will be at the rate of ten cents per mile less normal commuting costs or mileage from home to office to home. Expenses are approved by department management.

XIV. EMPLOYEE CHARGES

An employee or spouse of employee will be given rebate of commission on airline tickets for personal travel. This rebate will apply only to ticket or portion thereof for employee and/or spouse. (Rebate does note apply to any other member of employee's family.) Tickets may be charged in accordance with our regular credit policy which requires all accounts to be paid in full within thirty days. At employee's request, ticket costs may be charged through payroll deduction.

XV. SEVERANCE AND TERMINATION

A. COMPANY-INITIATED TERMINATION: If employment is terminated at the initiation of the company, severance pay will be provided on the basis of one week's pay for each year of full-time employment, up to a maximum of two weeks pay plus accrued vacation pay.

B. EMPLOYEE-INITIATED TERMINATION: If termination is initiated by the employee, notice should be given department management in accordance with guidelines established for company-initiated termination.

C. VACATION PAY UPON TERMINATION: After the first year of employment, vacation is earned in increments of six months full-time employment. Therefore, vacation pay upon termination will be based on six full months of employment after the employee anniversary date, with one week's pay being given for each six months of employment after that first anniversary date.

INDEX

The ABCs of Travel, 33
Administrative skill, 9, 64
Air Traffic Conference
   managerial accreditation by, 3, 22-24, 41
   reduced rate privileges of, 6, 34, 36, 38, 78
Air Traffic Conference Travel Agency Training Program, 31
Ambitions of job applicants, 9
American Society of Travel Agents, 30-32
Applicants
   appearance of, 5
   candor with, 4, 8
   checking references of, 11-17, 19
   establishing rapport with, 5
   evaluating the stability of, 18
   give and take with, 5-8
   job knowledge of, 17
   job satisfaction of, 17-18
   personal qualities of, 9-11, 18-19
   qualifications of, 2-3
   skills inventory checklist for, 2
   from travel schools, 19-21
Association of Retail Travel Agents, 32
Benefits
   explanation of, during interviews, 4, 6
   for reduced rate travel, 6, 34, 36, 38, 78-79
   See also Holiday policy; Sick days; etc.
Breech Training Academy, 30, 32
Certified Travel Counselor, 32
Checklists
   of applicant "red flags," 10-11
   for building morale, 46
   of desirable applicant skills, 2
   of employee training guidelines, 26-27

   of good supervisory traits, 65-66
   of job interview questions, 6-8
   for people problem management, 62
   of supervisory responsibilities, 67-68
Civil Rights Act of 1964, 42
Command, 51
Complaints, 57-59
Confidentiality, 14
Cost-of-living review, 34, 35
Courage, 64
Creative ability, 64
CTC. *See* Certified Travel Counselor
Decision making, 4, 17-19, 65
Delegation, 50, 65
Discrimination, 42-43
Employees. *See* Staff
Employment agencies, 3
Employment application
   of job applicants, 3-4
   of potential managers, 23
Employment history, 15, 18
Enthusiasm. *See* Positive mental attitude
Equal Employment and Opportunity Commission (EEOC), 42
Evaluation
   for applicant hiring, 17-19
   (*See also* Recruitment)
   of employee performance, 46-50
   for managerial self appraisal, 44, 69-74
Expense reimbursement, 78
Fair Labor Standards Act, 40-42
Familiarization trips, 6, 34, 38, 78
   excused absences for, 77

INDEX

and the Fair Labor Standards Act, 41-42
as part of benefits plan, 35-36
role of, in training, 29, 30
Firing. *See* Termination
Fiscal year, 75
Friendliness, 9
Full-time employee, 75
Funerals, 77
Hill, Napoleon, 74
Hiring. *See* Recruitment
Holiday policy, 36, 76
Honesty, 10
Incentive plans, 6, 34, 35
 budgeting for, 38
 distinguished from profit sharing, 38
 vesting in, 37
Individual Retirement Accounts (IRA), 36-37
Institute of Certified Travel Agents, 32
Insurance benefits, 6, 34, 35, 77-78
International Air Transport Association
 managerial accreditation by, 3, 22-24, 32, 41
 reduced rate privileges of, 6, 34, 36, 38, 78
Interviews
 regarding job performance, 48-49
 See also Job interview
Job description, 3
Job Interview
 backgrounding for, 3-4
 conclusion of, 8
 establishing rapport in, 5
 explaining your benefits package in, 4, 6
 preliminary stage of, 4
 question and answer period in, 5-8
Job interviewers, 8
Job knowledge, 17, 22
Job performance. *See* Staff, performance evaluations of
Job satisfaction, 17-18, 45
 breakdown of, 57-59
 and the problem employee, 59-62
Judgement, 65
Jury duty, 77
Leaves of absence, 77
Lehmann, Armin D., 32-33
Managers
 conference accreditations of, 3, 22-24, 32, 41
 crucial qualities for, 63-66
 definition of, 75
 disciplinary action by, 53, 56

instructional guidelines for, 26-27
interviewing questions for, 8
as morale builders, 43, 46
order giving by, 50-53
recruitment decision making by, 18-19
recruitment of, 22-24
responsibilities of, 66-68
self-evaluation by, 44, 69-74
and staff dissatisfaction, 57-62
Maternity leave, 77
Meetings, 28-29, 76
Military duty, 77
Minimum wage, 40
Morale, 43-46
OAG. *See* Official Airline Guide
Objectivity
 in disciplinary action, 54
 of references, 15
 in staff performance ratings, 47-48
Office hours, 75
Official Airline Guide, 28, 33
Orders
 components of, 51
 rules for, 52
 types of, 50-51
Overtime, 41-42, 77
Owners
 instructional guidelines for, 26-27
 relations of, with managers, 22-23, 68
Part-time employee, 75
Peale, Norman Vincent, 64
Positive mental attitude
 of applicants, 9
 and the manager's job, 63
Problem employees, 59-62
Productivity, 18
Profit sharing plans, 6, 34, 35, 78
 budgeting for, 38
 distinguished from incentives, 38
 examples of, 38-40
 vesting in, 37
Publications
 for professional education, 32-33
 about wage and hour laws, 43
Recruitment
 to avoid people problems, 1, 3, 61
 final evaluation in, 17-19
 job interviewing in, 3-8
 preliminaries in, 1-3
 reference checking in, 11-17, 19
 of travel agency managers, 22-24

of travel school graduates, 19-21
  See also Applicants
"Red flags," 10-11, 19
Reduced rate privileges, 6, 34, 36, 38, 78
Reference checking
  importance of, 11, 13
  of personal references, 17
  by telephone, 12-15
  in writing, 16-17
Re-hiring, 14-15
Reimbursement, 78
Reliability, 10, 18
Requests, 51
Résumés
  of job applicants, 3-4
  of potential managers, 23
Retirement programs, 36-37
Role-playing, 29
Salary, 34, 77
  payment of during familiarization trips, 35-36
  review of, 6, 34-35, 77
Satisfaction. *See* Job satisfaction
Selection. *See* Recruitment
Self-evaluation for managers, 44, 69-74
Self-motivation, 9
Serious offenses, 56
Severe offenses, 56
Sick days, paid, 34, 36, 76
Skills
  of job applicants, 2
  of travel managers, 63-66
Staff
  anniversary dates of, 75
  building morale in, 43-46, 55
  compensation of, 33-37
  complaints by, 57-59
  disciplining of, 53-56
  incentive and profit sharing plans for, 37-40
  indoctrination of, 25, 27
  managerial relations with, 67-68
  order giving to, 50-53
  performance evaluations of, 46-50, 55
  as problem employees, 59-62
  training of, 20, 25-33
  travel benefits of, 6, 34, 36, 38, 78-79
Stone, W. Clement, 64
Subordinates. *See* Staff
Suggestion, 51
Tardiness of job applicants, 5
Termination
  company policy toward, 79
  and employee offenses, 56
Training
  excused absences for, 77
  in familiarization trips, 29-30
  formal vs informal methods of, 25-26
  instructional guidelines for, 26-27
  meetings for, 28-29, 76
  on-the-job methods of, 27
  professional education in, 30-32
  publications for, 32-33
  role of orientation in, 27
  role-playing in, 29
Travel and Tourism (Lehmann), 33
Travel Marketing and Agency Management Guidelines (Lehmann), 32-33
Travel schools
  list of, 21
  recruitment from, 19-20
  for structured training, 30-32
Ultimatum, 53
Vacancy, 1
Vacation policy, 34, 36, 76, 79
Volunteers, 51
Warnings, 53
Wheaton Travel, Inc., 75